By Roy Blount, Jr.

———

*Not Exactly
What I Had
in Mind*

ROY BLOUNT, JR.

Not Exactly What I Had in Mind

The Atlantic Monthly Press
BOSTON / NEW YORK

FIRST EDITION

LIBRARY OF CONGRESS CATALOGING-IN-PUBLICATION DATA

Blount, Roy.
  Not exactly what I had in mind.

  1. United States—Social life and customs—
1971–   —Anecdotes, facetiae, satire, etc. I. Title.
E169.02B56   1985   973.927'0207   85-71411
ISBN 0-87113-031-9

Parts of this book have previously appeared in the following publications: *Advertising Age, Atlanta Weekly, The Atlantic, Esquire, Gentleman's Quarterly, Light Year '85, Mademoiselle, The Movies, New England Monthly, The New York Times, The New York Times Book Review, Playboy, Sports Illustrated, Vanity Fair.*

BP
Published simultaneously in Canada

PRINTED IN THE UNITED STATES OF AMERICA

This book
(but not the title)
is for my boy Johnny B.,
who can hit
and also sympathize

Contents

INTRODUCTION
Strings Attached

Jokes are so diverse that no one man can see them all.
— Max Beerbohm

Alas, mankind has yet to invent a system of relationships more natural than money.
— Vassily Aksyonov

... and I'm an immaterial girl.
— Miss Liberty, just before leaping into the harbor and swimming off

---

I F the title of this book strikes you as ... picky, well, I know what you mean. I have half a mind to break down, plunge into the eighties, and write something heartier, called *Greed Works.* Do you think I *like* being out of touch with American values? Not long ago I climbed up into the Statue of Liberty's head. It felt good in there, and I thought rousing thoughts.

What a woman! Embosomer of Einstein, Garbo, and Jelly Roll Morton. *And* Jesse Helms. When her cornerstone was laid, *Huckleberry Finn* was at the printers. Not being Jesse Helms, I don't presume to know exactly what she has in mind. But I have a hard time believing that America today is it.

And she undoubtedly *likes* capitalism, within reason. So do I. Back before money went crazy, my daddy was president of the national organization of savings and loans. He bankrolled homes for a living. I aim to prosper in my own small business, trying to turn a dollar making unencumbered sense. In an ideal system, I'm afraid I would find myself writing for the common good, as determined by the kind of people who like to serve on committees.

Say somebody in a bow tie were to knock on my door and announce, "You don't have to mess with the marketplace anymore! Just sign here and you get a stipend from the Universal League of Free Expression, renewable annually so long as you swear to operate only in terms of high purpose." It would sound fishy to me. I don't trust clean money. An American isn't after a free ride, if he can help it. He wants to sail his own boat, which means getting a grip on the strings attached.

And that's where an American is onto something fundamental. According to the *New York Times,* which has my implicit trust on anything to do with nature's building blocks, scientists are beginning to believe that everything in the universe, including airplane food and Albania, is made of strings. Here are the details of this hypothesis, as I understand them:

Nature boasts not just four dimensions but *ten* (or nine more than Ronald Reagan). Everything is arranged not just symmetrically but *super*symmetrically. There are a lot of new subatomic particles, called squarks, sleptons (which would explain the way my hair looks in the morning), hadrons (no, *hadrons*), gluons, and photinos. And the gluons hold all the others together in strings. And the scientist who got started thinking along these lines was called Theodor F. E. Kaluza.

And I'm willing to believe it.

I wouldn't be surprised if there turns out to be even *more* to the universe. (These new dimensions, now. Would they be something we've heard of? Hope, chewiness? Or would they be hard to describe: something halfway between height and time; something that's sort of like width only with more brio and it tastes a little like dark meat of chicken?) When my son John was five he asked me, "Does the world have everything in the world in it?" *Yes.* Although it's hard to comprehend. Who would ever have thought there would be a man called Theodor F. E. Kaluza? And that's just the world. In the universe, there is no telling what all, I'll bet. A squark may have some manner of farms and weather and TV shows inside it; and way on off in the other direction there may be things that think of *us* as new particles. For all we know they call us niblets, say — not having any idea what that means in our language.

Now. How do we square this with Ronald Reagan's sense of reality? We square it by bearing in mind that Ronald Reagan makes many Americans feel good.

But so do drugs, in the short run. Cocaine makes you feel like you've got the world on a string because it makes you feel like you have cut through all the real strings. When I think of the strings attached to Reaganism, my mind turns to the federal deficit. Surely we would not be in such great financial shape if we weren't $200 billion in the hole. So I think it is incumbent upon us, as Americans, to *feel like* we are a fifth of a trillion short. It's not easy; but then it's no snap to take cognizance of the purple mountain majesties, either.

Maybe I am tied to some kind of old-fashioned symmetry. But I can't help thinking that eventually we are going to have to dig up that $200 billion somewhere. And I don't want the Treasury Department to be scratching around at the last minute, reduced to desperate measures. Holding an international raffle, hundred million bucks a ticket, winner gets his face carved on Mount Rushmore. Maybe it wouldn't be so bad if it's the CEO of one of our own defense contractors — even though he would presumably tack the $100 million (promotional expenses) onto his next bill to the government. But what if it's some relative of the late Shah who lives in Gstaad and has little bitty rabbit teeth and a pencil-thin mustache, or the Reverend Sun Myung Moon, or the head of a South American government's Bureau de Coca? And how many people are there, worldwide, outside of Miami (where they probably don't want a high profile), who can put their hands on that kind of cash today? Say there are a couple of thousand. That just adds up to $20 billion, that's a drop in the bucket. And wait a minute: don't forget the expense of the carving. That kind of work today, you're lucky to get it done for a couple of billion, even if you throw in a free chance in the drawing for the sculptor. Then you've got administrative costs. Plus legal fees — some heir of Teddy Roosevelt sues for infringement. Before you know it you're only clearing six, seven billion. But the main problem, I think, is it's tacky.

But then, what do I know. Ronald Reagan is the most widely beloved American since E.T., and I have trouble believing he *exists*.

On the question of whether he truly stands for something, here's what Ronald Reagan told Tom Wicker in 1978: "One thing I learned as an actor. You can't come over on the camera unless you really believe the lines you're speaking."

In other words, Reagan in 1939 really believed the lines of an ineffectual drunk (*Dark Victory*); in 1940 he really believed the lines of an exemplary fullback (*Knute Rockne, All American*); in 1942 he really believed the lines of a liberal college professor (*Bedtime for Bonzo*); in 1957 he really believed the lines of a hard-ass naval commander (*Hellcats of the Navy*); in 1964 he really believed the lines of an assassin who knocks Angie Dickinson flat (*The Killers*); and in 1985 he really believes the lines of a Clint-Eastwood-with-affability who regards a blood-soaked faction in Nicaragua as "the moral equivalent of our Founding Fathers," who observes that Nazi war dead were no less victimized than concentration-camp martyrs, and who adds, "Yes, I know all the bad things that happened in that war. I was in uniform four years myself" (in California, making films).

Lines, in that sense, are different from strings, in the nature-of-physical-reality sense. But I think Reagan does stand for something. He reminds me of Elvis. "If I could ever find a white boy who could sing like a nigger," the man who first recorded Elvis had said, "I could make a million dollars." I think Ronald Reagan caught the eye of a lot of people who, in the same spirit (adjusted for inflation), were looking for a true believer who could grin (and sweeten the pot) like a liberal.

Years ago I left my home in Georgia, at the risk of losing touch with precious gluons of oral resonance, because in Georgia I sensed a too-shameless concentration of people who loved to fulminate against Russia and smut, who felt it was pusillanimous to survey the world from any other point of view than that of the eagle on the dollar, and who seemed to feel not only high-minded but even tingly when they looked upon the Pentagon as a case of pure need and upon fatherless babies in the ghetto as cases of threateningly unbridled self-interest. And all this in the name of Jesus.

As far as I can tell, Ronald Reagan is one of those people. Only without the oral resonance.

"Those people." A dangerous phrase. Those people *we* aren't tied to. You don't hear Miss Liberty using that phrase. "It takes all kinds," you hear her saying, with relish. I don't get the feeling that Ronald Reagan agrees with her.

I think that Ronald Reagan thinks that those forces, and his smile, and a wealth of imaginary capital, are all America needs. When elements clash with what he has in mind, he sees no reason why those elements shouldn't disappear.

You can tell that from his jokes. He jokes about dropping bombs on Russia and exporting dissatisfied farmers. To uncooperative Congressmen he says, "Make my day," which is what Clint Eastwood (who couldn't tie John Wayne's shoes) says when he is itching to blow some punk away. When Reagan was governor of California, and Patty Hearst's kidnappers were demanding that free canned goods be distributed to ghetto dwellers, he said it would be a good time for an epidemic of botulism. I don't get those jokes. I am not *about* to get them. If you ask me, jocularity ought to get down and strum the all-but-inconceivable strings that bind the whole range of Miss Liberty's children (okay, so she's not married; she doesn't need to be made an honest woman) supersymmetrically together. This book is not about Ronald Reagan *per se* (whatever that might mean). But what I have in mind, roughly speaking, is to pull against the President's sense of humor without losing hold of mine.

> *Well we know we're not exactly what we have in mind,*
> *But that's how things tend to go, I find.*
> *The mind's got a job to do and so do we.*
> *Lord have mercy on reality.*

Talking Wrenches

What You Personally Can Do about the Federal Deficit

THERE are economists who say, "Hey, don't worry about it. It's not, you know, *money*, as you know it."

There are economists who say, "It will mean — unless real, drastic, structural steps are taken by next fiscal Thursday — that Arabs will own your grandchildren."

All I know is, it is $200 billion. Or $175 billion. Around in there. And it is America's. Which means it is mine.

And I am not going to just sit here.

I am going to think of something the individual American citizen can do to reduce it.

Here is what I have thought of:

Buy stamps and throw them away.

If you go to your local post office and try to give the person at the window twenty dollars and ask him to forward it on up to the person in charge of balancing the federal books, he will be nonplussed. If, however, you buy a roll of twenty-cent stamps and throw them away, you will have pumped twenty dollars into the federal government without requiring it to do anything except print those stamps and sell them to you. The federal government comes out, I don't know, $19.40 ahead.

And no one is hurt.

Another thing you might do is travel to Russia, find a Soviet citizen willing to pair off with you, and send to the Department of Defense an affidavit signed by you and that Soviet citizen (call her Olga Petrova) to the effect that the two of you have declared a mutual nonaggression pact and therefore you authorize the federal government to reduce military outlays by whatever it costs to defend you against Olga Petrova. But that would take something out of the pockets of people who happen to be employed by our military-industrial complex.

Throwing away stamps doesn't disadvantage anyone. Mailmen are not deprived of any business, because you are still sending the same amount of mail. In point of fact, the stamp-production complex makes *more* money — so that all the people employed by it can better afford to buy stamps and throw them away. You see how this thing — antiphilately, we might call it — could gather momentum.

Okay. It bothers you to buy anything and throw it away. I can understand that. So here is a fallback position: put twenty-cent stamps on postcards. An extra six cents to the federal government on each postcard mailed. It adds up.

Or you can do this: you can leave an entire new roll of stamps on your windowsill with the window open, allowing sudden rainfall to stick the whole roll together.

That is what I did recently. And I saw the downside of it. I tried to peel the roll apart. I produced stamp clumps, stamp ghosts, stamp shreds.

What a stupid, wasteful thing to do! Was I hacked off.

But then I looked at the upside. I had reduced the federal deficit.

You see how ideas like this are born?

Of course if you do a little arithmetic, it looks like every American will have to throw away five thousand twenty-cent stamps in order to eliminate the deficit entirely. (Now that the cost of sending a letter has gone up to twenty-two cents, there are probably a lot of twenties left over.) That's twenty

4

thousand stamps for a family of four. So there might be great whuffling clumps of loosened stamp rolls blowing through the nation's streets like tumbleweed. Still, that's better than picturing your granddaughter as a harem girl.

P.S. It has been objected that — because the post office is no longer a part of the federal government, but is run by an independent company catchily known as the United States Postal Service — this proposal will not work. But it is mine and I am sticking with it. Why does no one ever pick apart the ideas of Ronald Reagan? I'll tell you why: because he owes everyone too much money.

How to High-Falute

PERSONALLY I like a good, solid, family-style restaurant that has a name like Rip and Emma's and is presided over by Emma, who on a slow night will sit down with you while she shells peas. She'll call you honey and point out the picture of the late Rip with his accordion and tell you about the time he ran for mayor and his opponent called him a liar and Rip came right back and called his opponent a liar and they attempted to resolve the issue by taking public lie-detector tests but they both passed so they tried again and they both failed; so Rip played his accordion and sang his campaign song, which was to the tune of "Blessed Assurance." At this kind of restaurant, you get seated and served right away as long as you look like a fairly nice person and your nose isn't running.

But I realize that there are people who prefer swanker places. Eateries called Magna Carta or Le Foie Engorgé, which do not encourage the appetite of anyone who has not just come from racquetball with Cap Weinberger. And everybody looks at you as if you probably don't know how to eat *caniche vinaigrette avec toute la sauce* without getting it all over yourself.

Some feel that the only way to be received and waited upon with any degree of enthusiasm at a restaurant like that is to walk in with one of the Bouvier sisters on your arm and a fifty-dollar bill plastered to your forehead. Not so.

Oh, it's one way. It will *work* — at least until March 1988, when some analysts expect good tables to jump as high as both Bouviers, three twenties, and a platinum tooth.

But more and more people today are trying less traditional approaches. For instance:

Becoming the Chef

Ferrell Trivet had always wanted to dine at Le Haut Falutin, in Manhattan. Whenever he tried to gain admittance, however, the maître d' sprayed paraquat on him and sent him away.

Ferrell tried humor: "If you spray me with defoliant, how do you expect me to *leave?*" But the maître d' had heard that one before. So Ferrell said to himself, "I know what. I'll become the chef."

Easier said than done. First there were the inevitable dues-paying years at a live sushi counter on Staten Island. Then at an S and M sushi bar in Queens. Then at a place — whose location Ferrell refuses to disclose because he doesn't want to "bring it one dime's worth of patronage more than, may God cease to avert his eyes, it attracts already" — where he was forced to prepare baby-seal sashimi.

Even when, at last, he got through the portals of Le Haut Falutin's kitchen, it was not as chef. Oh no. It was not even as *sous*-chef. At the age of forty-seven, Ferrell was expected to perform as *saucier*.

Part of the job was congenial to him, although debilitating. It is well known that chefs — like all creative people — can get to hitting the sauce so hard that they turn bright red and scuttle sluggishly around on the floor like nearly done lobsters making a break for it. It is the saucier's job to do roughly two-thirds of the chef's tippling — which, depending on the size and intensity of the chef, can be fatal and nearly always causes disorientation, even in Chinese places. Still, Ferrell did not mind.

It was the other half of the saucier's role that Ferrell never warmed to: walking past the tables in a mauve-and-magenta uniform, making snippy remarks to the customers and tossing his head. Intellectually, he knew this was essential in such a fancy place. But in his heart he craved customerhood for himself so fondly that he derived no pleasure from making it unpleasant for the favored few who were able to attain it.

Then one day the chef keeled over permanently, and as it happened he landed on the *sous*-chefs, although they had been warned repeatedly not to hover. And poof: Ferrell was entitled to a big white hat and imperious ways.

Now he was cooking. But not yet dining. He would race through his duties, hop into evening wear, and dash round to the front entrance, only to be told, *"Je regrette, mais la* kitchen is closed." Catch-22.

To make matters worse, the maître d' would come back to the kitchen and taunt him: "Eh, Chef Ferrell, how come you nevair take a table, eh? Oo-ha-ha. You no like *le* coo-keeng, eh? Heh-heh-hehhhh."

Then one evening, as Ferrell was stirring just the right amounts of cockle-muscle extract, minced mussel cocks, and *les petites choses inquiétantes et maladroites de la mer* into the *bouillabaisse polonaise,* he paused, inhaled the bouquet, gazed fondly into the vat, and realized he didn't need a table. He could eat all the *bouillabaisse* he wanted. So he did. The whole vat.

And he left Le Haut Falutin, adopted his saucier (whom he allowed to wear Levi's and required to be fresh but civil), and opened his own place that is all kitchen: patrons are charged a *prix fixe* (eighty-five dollars, lunch; whatever Ferrell feels like charging, dinner) to wander from pot to pot stirring, inhaling, and tasting.

Dressing Up Like Michael Jackson

The bad news: headwaiters are catching on to this one. You'll have to field a stiff battery of questions to prove that you can talk the way Michael Jackson actually does when he is out with his high-life crowd:

"Why do you wear that glove?"

"I got this from Mickey Mouse. Only he has to wear two of them because nobody wants to see mouse fingers."

"Are you, in fact, Diana Ross?"

"No, you're thinking of Carl Lewis, who is Grace Jones."

"Were you just born knowing how to move like that?"

"No. It's from high-school football. I was at an inside linebacker slot, see, and this pulling guard came at me, about two hundred thirty pounds and going *hunhf*-uffa, *hunhf*-uffa, and I thought to myself, How'm I going to show him I'm *bad?* So I did this little spin, you know, um ch'coot'n — wooo — ch'ch'ch'ch'cootn'-*pah:* unh! And he missed me. And he still does."

Lowering Your Expectations

What is so *wrong,* really, about a table situated so that the bartender has to be constantly reminded not to forget himself and dry his hands on your dinner companion's hair? In some parts of the world, people eat bugs.

Sponge Baths on the Way Over in the Taxi

Restaurant service personnel are extraordinarily sensitive to what scientists call phewomones: tiny (it goes without saying, tiny, but I mean *truly* tiny) ionized particles that are given off by the skin and moist membranes of people who are not quality. A recent study showed that whereas the average person cannot sniff out unpalatable people without the aid of visual clues such as wristwatches obviously costing less than $1,500, the average career waiter can do it blindfolded and while eating yesterday's bait.

Getting Physical

Baird Roxie is not particularly built, knows no martial arts, and does not want any trouble. But he can handle himself in a restaurant. When he is welcomed by an icy look, he seizes the headwaiter by the scruff of the neck in such a stringent way that it includes the Adam's apple. Then in a calm, firm voice he says, "I'm Mr. Roxie and here's my major credit card, which as you see does not expire until 9/87. When I turn loose of your neck, I'd like you to say hidy graciously to Jennalynn Russet, as fine a woman as you'd ever want to meet. And then I want you to walk us on over to a comfortable table. And then I want you to go tell your sommelier not to come high-nosing over here with a wine list that looks like an album of wallpaper samples but just to bring us some of your house red, which ought to be fine if the house is worth a shit."

Baird Roxie always gets good service. It helps to be accompanied by Jennalynn Russet, who is perfectly willing to crouch behind the headwaiter so he can be floored by a slight push on the chest, if necessary.

Affecting Extreme Nonchalance

While chewing a toothpick (which suggests that you may have eaten already) and wearing a feather in your hatband, stand out on the restaurant's doorstep, facing the street. Rock back and forth from heels to toes, contentedly, and hum a tune such as "If You've Got the Money, I've Got the Time."

After a while, the door will open slightly.

Pretend not to notice.

It will close.

Continue to rock and hum.

The door will open again, slightly wider. An eye will be visible.

Don't pay any attention.

The door will close again.

Keep on humming and rocking.

Finally, the door will open enough for the headwaiter to stick his head out, which he will do. In a moment, he will speak:

"I say."

You look around. Regard the headwaiter's head as if try-ing to determine whether you have seen it anywhere before. Shake your own head: You haven't. Face the street again.

"I *say*," says the headwaiter.

Look around again. "Sorry, stranger, I don't believe I know you."

"Well! I am this establishment's headwaiter!"

"That a fact? I'm Corky Severingham, from Lake Waste, Arkansas." Resume humming. This time the door is slammed. But after a few seconds it opens again.

"I say! Am I to infer that you are interested in dining at this establishment?"

"Hm? Oh, no, thanks, I don't think I'd . . . Okay."

Several people come dashing up the sidewalk. "And this is my wife Pepper and her brother Treat and his wife Ro-sareece and these four are the babies, they'll need high chairs, but Treat and Rosareece's boy Toomey there just needs a bib and a bowl of applesauce, and the same goes for Momma's aunt Mae April here. Momma couldn't come her-self, she's got a board meeting back home, but she asked us to bring her some of those real thin crackers. Let's see — nine, ten, eleven, and take away Momma — that's ten of us, but we'll need a table for twelve because we like to have a busboy sit on either side of this batch of little ones here and kind of keep 'em down to an uproar. Now don't you go rear-ranging a lot of tables for us; we'll do that. . . ."

Meanwhile there is no way the headwaiter can grab all that many people of different sizes, so at least two-thirds of you will get in. "My good man!" the headwaiter will cry. "We couldn't possibly accommodate all these people!"

"Oh. Well. I tell you what we'll do. Just Pepper and I'll take a table for two — make it for three. Great-aunt Mae April don't want to eat anything, but she'd like to sit there and look around. And the rest can all go on down to the Chock Full O' Nuts — they like that better anyway. Oh, I see Great-aunt Mae April has already found us a table. We don't even need to bother you. But I appreciate your interest."

Going In with a Seeing Eye Dog

Once I was at a cocktail party when a very successful unsighted stockbroker came in with her dog, which went right over to the coffee table and ate a nice Brie and two dozen bacon-wrapped water chestnuts. No one said anything. Pretty much anything a Seeing Eye dog does, it does quietly, so its master either doesn't notice or need not admit to noticing, and it can get away with it.

In a restaurant, the dog will take care of everything. It will silently clamp its jaws on the maître d's ankle. The maître d' will hop around and wear an expression of outrage, but if he says anything at all it will probably be no more than "M'sieu! Your dog!"

"Ah yes, Shiva," you say. "I don't know what I would do without her."

Shiva will then lead the headwaiter and you to whatever table she chooses. If people are dining there already — as may well be the case, since a dog prefers a table with food on it — Shiva will seize each diner in turn by the ankle until they all leave. Then she will clean their plates, and both of you will be sitting pretty.

Just be sure not to cry out "WHAT!?" until someone *tells* you the size of the check.

It will be noted that this essay has dealt primarily with fancy restaurants' *first* line of defense. That is because, once you have fought your way past the greeter, it is a simple matter to dispel regular waitpersons' antagonism. You just raise your voice every so often to say "national talent search," "some lucky unknown," "we've *got* Meryl and Warren already, that's not the problem," and "a new face for the second lead." Unless this is such a deluxe place that it doesn't hire show people but only dyspeptic foreign men. In that case you bring along one of those surf-casting reels, a good treble hook, and plenty of line. Eighty-pound test is plenty strong enough, since dyspeptic foreign men seldom jump high enough to bring their entire weight into play.

But how do you get them close enough to hook them? Well, my friend Jim Seay, the poet, says, "One of the things that separate class from trash is what kind of bait you use." I like to cast one of Emma's blueberry muffins. See, the reason waiters in high-dollar places are dyspeptic is that they are never around any good, solid, family-style food that fairly nice people can afford.

That's what I meant earlier when I said something about restaurant service personnel eating yesterday's bait. I meant things on the order of Emma's blueberry muffins. What did you think I meant? Spring lizards? Hey, restaurant service personnel are human beings. The only reason some of them turn mean is that they have to work in places where everybody just played racquetball with Cap Weinberger.

I Had to Get into It with a Wrench

I GOT myself one of these talking wrenches. Even though I see it as a bad trend, things taking on the power of speech. Cars talk, cameras talk, even airports talk:

"This — miracle — electronic — passenger — shuttle — will — be — delayed. Some — person — has — interfered — with — the — proper — closing — of — the — perfectly — calibrated — doors. Unless — that — person — removes — all — portions — of — him — or — herself — from — the — doorway — we — will — sit — here — until — every — flight — has — departed. It — is — all — the — same — to — me. This — miracle . . ."

Why doesn't anybody come up with cars, cameras, airports that *listen?*

It used to be, you heard from insentient objects only in writing. Sign on a Laundromat washing machine: "I Am Out of Order. Please Use One of My Buddies." Once I was served a baked potato with a little triangular cardboard notice stuck in it that said, "I Have Been Rubbed, Tubbed, and Scrubbed. You May Eat My Jacket."

But we've moved on beyond that, today. I understand the National Tuber Council is developing a baked potato, for fern bars, that addresses the diner aloud:

"Hello. My — name — is — Tatum — and — I — am — your — choice — of — potato — for — the — evening. May — I — suggest — that — the — best — part — of — me — is — my — . . ."

Jacket! In a baked potato's mealy little mouth, at least butter would melt. What kind of person, the potato may sense, would go ahead and eat an entity that says, "You may eat my jacket"? Jimmy Carter on TV was a talking baked potato. Ronald Reagan is a talking siphon (of juices into coffers), ageless, impermeable; and he thrives.

Machines are calm; they don't raise their voices; they have no shame. What are you going to do? Yell, "Don't take that tone with me"? The machine is programmed to reply, "This — tone — is — based — upon — thorough — testing. It — is — designed — to — be — ingratiating. If — you — are — not — ingratiated — you — are — not — statistically — relevant."

And yet I bought a talking wrench.

I'll tell you why.

I can use a little guidance when I'm handling a wrench. Especially when I'm reaching up underneath something at an awkward angle. I get turned around. Straining away at an intractable nut, I stop and think: "Am I just making this tighter?" And once I stop and think, I am lost. Left, right, clockwise, counterclockwise run together like worms in a bucket. And I lie there thinking, in an ever-widening swirl, of all the different ways in which my life needs direction. My heart wrenches. I don't know which way to turn.

Then too, I like the word *wrench*. Good straightforward Anglo-Saxon, sounds like what it means. (In a deep structural, hard-to-hear way, I register the *w*.) Compare *semiconductor*. Which is it, then: does it conduct or doesn't it conduct?

There is something not just handy but also hand-in-hand about a wrench. How do we stop a mechanical scheme that staggers human scale? We throw a monkey wrench into it. A spanner in the works. Might it be feasible to "turn" (in the counterintelligence sense) a talking wrench?

At first I just kept the new wrench on top of the refrigerator, and acted naturally around it. When kitchen conversation came round to high technology, I would speak my mind. Then I'd take the wrench down, show it to people. "I respect a good wrench," I'd say. "Nice heft to it. What kind of heft you think there is to a semiconductor?" I didn't address the wrench. I was waiting until we had something to talk about.

Then one day, taking apart the bottom of the dishwasher to find out what was clogging it up, I got into a wheels-within-wheels situation: one thing that loosened in one direction, inside another thing that seemed to loosen in the other direction or at least shouldn't be loosened until the other thing was loosened, and beneath both things was some other fixture that was threaded into a socket even more profound, and beneath that was probably something that if I ever got down to it (not that I wanted to) would turn the whole kitchen. And all of these things were under viscid water. I groped around in there with the wrench, and got a purchase, and tugged, and nothing happened. And I stopped to think. And here came that old vertigo.

"*Am I going in the wrong direction?*" I said out loud.

"Mfrlg," said the wrench.

I disengaged it and brought it up.

"Flplfph," it said. "Yeah."

"I am? Going in the wrong direction?"

"If you ask me. Course if you want to go on ahead and start breaking and stripping and binding up things within things within things . . . "

"No!" I said. "This is exactly the reason I got . . . you. I'm always — "

"So go the other direction," the wrench said. "Ain't but two."

16

"Right," I said. I stuck the wrench back down in there and felt its jaws catch hold. And I turned the other direction, *hard*, with *faith*.

"Nnnng," I said.

"Nnnn-nnng," said the wrench.

"Nnnn-*nnnng*," I said.

"Mfrlgph," said the wrench.

I extricated it.

"You realize," the wrench went on after a moment, "there's such a thing as a talking dishwasher. With talking components. As it is, I got nobody to check anything out with down there."

"I'd be afraid a talking dishwasher would sing," I said. " 'Swish, swash, wushy wishes, / Swish, swash, do the dishes.' I don't want that."

"Uh-huh. Well, that's up to you. All I know is, we are going the right way."

"Hey, that's a big help," I said. "Shall we try it again?"

And we did.

"Nnnnng," I went. "Nnnnn-*ng.*"

"Nnnnn-nn-nnnnn-*nng*," went the wrench, and then the dishwasher, for all that it was nonspeaking, said:

"Flllllpppplplpl . . . pllp."

And all the viscid water ran out.

"Fwew," said the wrench.

"Hey," I exclaimed. "That went fine. Yes sir. Now I can feel around and clear out whatever was the obstruction. Fish head or something."

What I found was two pieces of glass, a swatch of peach skin, half a raw green bean, and something I couldn't identify at first.

"Oh. You know what I think this is?" I said. "A chicken tendon."

"You get ready to tighten back up," the wrench said, "let me know."

"All right," I said. "Let's do it." And we did.

"Well!" I said. "Listen, I've enjoyed working with you. You, uh, want to take a break?"

No response.

So I sat there on the kitchen floor with the wrench.

And then I just came on out with it:

"I've . . . always had problems with machines."

"Uh-huh," said the wrench after a moment.

"And, uh, with . . . tools."

"Uh-*huh*," said the wrench.

"With any kind of — I don't know what the collective term would be. I don't want to say 'gadget.' Some people would say . . . 'gizmo,' quote-unquote."

If the wrench took offense, it gave no sign.

"But I'm not out to pigeonhole. Is there any *insight* you could offer me?"

"I don't get into that," said the wrench.

"Oh. Uh-huh. But I was just thinking. Let me tell you a story. I used to work on a newspaper with a guy named Dick Link. And he used to write these great short editorials. We called them Linklets."

Wrench didn't say anything.

"Give you an example. In the first paragraph, Link takes note that a special state commission on education has just weighed in with a report. The commission declares that it has pinpointed a major problem: there are too many teachers in the state who aren't up to par. Right? Here is Link's second and final paragraph:

" 'Okay, all you bad teachers! Come on!' "

Not a peep from the wrench.

"So," I said. "The only reason I bring all this up is — one day Link and I walked by the composing room Coke machine. And someone had stuck a note on it. You know how people will do."

"Not really," said the wrench.

"Well, they will. Stick notes on machines. Or at least they used to, before machines talked. Anyway, here's what the note on the Coke machine said:

" 'This machine owes me thirty-five cents.'

"See. And . . . the point I'm coming to: Link, who *thought* in Linklets — Link took out a pencil and . . . People will do that. See something written on a wall or somewhere, they'll add a comment.

"So," I went on, "here's what Link wrote:

" 'As if a machine could owe.' "

Silence from the wrench.

"Was what he wrote," I said. " 'As if . . . a machine could owe.' And . . . I just wondered —"

"Hey," said the wrench.

And there was something so dismissive in the tone.

"Tell me about it," said the wrench.

I just sat there. I looked at the wrench.

"Great!" I said. "Thanks a lot! I need irony from a wrench!"

I glared at the wrench.

"Listen. You think I *enjoy* sitting here opening up to a damn *wrench?* Huh? But *you* can't unbend a bit, can you? *You* aren't interested in chicken tendons. *You* don't want to hear any Linklets. You're no different from any other hunk of gimmickry! Contraption! Doohickey! *Thingamajig!*"

A moment passed. Then:

"My — head — has — been — immersed — in — viscid — water. Please — blow — hot — dry — air — into — my — wiring — cavity — now. Failure — to — do — so — will — result — in — corrosion — of — my — communications — circuitry. The — choice — is — yours."

Mine. Mine! Why is it always *mine?*

How to Pack It All In

WHEN packing for a trip, bear this principle in mind: it is better, in a public place like an airport, to be bedraggled than naked. If you squeeze all your clothes into a carry-on bag — I don't care if it *is* so cannily constructed, according to the airline-magazine ads, that you can live out of it for the rest of your life — your clothes are going to get wadded up. And you will look as if you have been raiding the Goodwill collection box.

But if you take several pieces of proper luggage that have to be checked, the airline will lose them, and your one set of clothes will become so vile in a few days that in all decency you will be forced to travel nude.

I don't know why airlines always lose checked baggage. You would think they might at least warn you, as they are briskly slapping on tags, that "it is the policy of this airline that we have no earthly idea where we are checking these bags through to." But they don't. They behave for all the world as if they were flying your luggage to your destination.

But when you reach that place, you will stand sweatily, anxiously, among the teeming, shouldering masses at the conveyor belt for an hour or so while skis, pineapples, caged weimaraners, duffel bags marked WARNING, kayaks, bass viols, and mysterious large trapezoidal crates belonging to *someone* click-clack past, but your own bags will not appear. So you will go to the baggage-service desk, where a semi-functionary considerably less apologetic than Richard Nixon will give you a long form to fill out. Or you may elect to save the form and wear it the following day. The baggage-service person does not find it remarkable, does not see it as any business of his, or of yours, that his airline has lost your property. "These things happen," he may say, if you insist on his saying something. If you rave and fume, the upshot will be that your only shirt gets sweatier sooner.

So you must pack everything in a carry-on bag. Now, I see some people walking through airports with trim, flat carry-on bags. These are presumably the same people who carry wafer-thin wallets. My own wallet — perhaps because it holds my entire fortune, and also "What to Do in Case of Sunstroke," and also the card of a police detective I met one night in Indianapolis (if I ever throw these out, I will get sunstroke *and* be arrested in Indianapolis within twenty-four hours) — looks like a camel's snout. My carry-on bag looks like a greatly enlarged bacon cheeseburger on a sesame roll with extra onions.

If your business, like mine, tends to take you from Hartford to Detroit via Richmond, Virginia; St. Paul, Minnesota; and Jackson, Mississippi, you will need to bring along an overcoat, a heavy suit, a light jacket, shorts, snow boots, sneakers, long underwear, flip-flops, canned heat, bug repellent, and a hat with earflaps. And six shirts. And some pants that will go with either the light jacket or the suit coat. And some wool socks and some thin socks. And a pair of gloves. And a briefcase, and some papers that won't fit into the briefcase, and a typewriter. And a book, in case you have read every novel about mad dogs haunting a seventeenth-century Scottish manse available in the airport shop. And some decongestant pills so your head cold won't be driven into your inner ears by cabin pressure. Also eight or nine dif-

ferent toiletries (you can, and will, leave some of these behind and purchase replacements in a hotel shop, but you
should bear in mind that they will cost $13.95 per tube).

So if you have a king-size bed at home, you spread all
these things out on it and then unzip all the zippers on your
carry-on bag and spread it out alongside. Then you step
back, survey the prospect, and wonder whether it might be
possible just to roll the whole prospect up, mattress and all,
and carry that aboard; or whether it might be possible to stay
home. But no. Neither thing is possible. You have miles to
go before you . . .

Well, a little nap would be refreshing. There was a study
in the paper the other day showing that people pack better
when they are rested. But there is no room on the bed. Be-
sides, your plane leaves in an hour and fourteen minutes, and
the airport is forty minutes away, and you haven't bought
your ticket yet.

So! Let's get packing. First get the cat out of the socks.
Now! Let's get down to it.

Say your carry-on bag is of the folded-over hanging vari-
ety, with lots of pockets. Those little pockets look easy. Put a
tie in each one. You really need only one tie, but there are
four of those little pockets; so put a tie in each one of them.
That's a start.

Now. Get the cat out of the socks again.

Now. Large hanging items. Sport coats, shirts. These
must be laid carefully, smoothly, the arms folded over just so,
in the large cavity where the coat hangers are.

Where the coat hangers were.

Where are the coat hangers?

You find some coat hangers, but they are not the same
ones that came with this bag; they are the ones that came
with a previous bag that exploded in Des Moines. So they
don't quite hook on to the little hook-on thing right. So you
have to bend their little hooks. And the little hook-on thing.
So you know they are going to come loose.

Still, you load several changes of clothes onto the hangers and work the whole mass somehow into the large cavity. And try to zip it up. It is like trying to zip three Serbian trappers into the same sleeping bag. So you figure you'll get it completely zipped later, after you've loaded the pockets on the other side. So you turn the bag over and start loading those pockets with miscellanea. But arms are flopping out of the large cavity. So you turn the bag back over, and everything you have loaded into the pockets falls out, including the cat.

But you get the whole thing pulled together. Oh yes, yes you do. You curse, and you kick, and you forget to put in any underwear, but you do get the whole thing pulled together. Because you are an American traveling person, and if you give up and stay home you will have to do something even worse than traveling, like straightening out your life.

Getting your stuff together, of course, does not mean being able to lift it. You have to jettison something. Ties. That's why we put extra ties in to begin with. Ties are easy to jettison. Jettisoning a jacket, say, would mean going back into the major cavity again, and the stuff in the major cavity has begun to swell visibly.

Now you can lift it. You can carry it out to the car. You can drive it to the airport. And you can drag it through the parking lot and all the way to the ticket counter. And by then your bag's contents have rearranged themselves into shifting, ill-balanced clumps that cause other travelers to stare.

So — partly to cut down on the number of times you will lurch into walls between ticket counter and gate, and partly so that people will no longer suspect you of transporting nearly suffocated chimpanzees — you do a little unzipping and repacking. Before you know it, your white shirt has stuck to the heel of a hurried traveler, and he is dragging it off toward the Green Concourse, and people are sneering at your wardrobe, and you discover that your athlete's-foot powder has come open and coated everything in your Dopp kit, including notably your toothbrush, and your deodorant stick is rolling off toward the newsstand. And — oh-h, surprise! — there is the cat.

You can deal with all this, though. You are a seasoned traveler. And you are on the first leg of your trip. Your bag hasn't split open yet and its handle hasn't come loose at one end yet and its main zipper hasn't jammed yet and shirts that you spilled beer on haven't gotten mingled in with the other shirts yet and you haven't acquired any keepsakes yet.

Keepsakes can be a problem. In the course of your travels, you will pick up gifts for loved ones back home — hats, conch shells, wooden airplanes that do loops if they aren't broken. And if you pass through Tennessee or Georgia, you will want to pick up a couple of bottles of Lem Motlow whiskey, which is a younger, cheaper, and I be damned if not better-tasting version of Jack Daniel's and is available in only those two states. If you get down into south Georgia during May or June, you'll want to get some Vidalia onions. If you're in New Orleans, you had better grab a couple of Dixie beers to take back with you; in Milwaukee you may score a wurst; and you might come by a comical alligator poster in Tampa and a cactus in Tucson. Let's face it, you can't get these things at home.

You won't be able to get every one of these things into your carry-on bag. So you'll acquire several auxiliary tote bags and will begin to resemble the baseball pitcher Satchel Paige at the age of seven, when he got his nickname hustling baggage at a railroad depot in Mobile. "I rigged up ropes around my shoulders and waist," Paige once said, "and I carried a satchel in each hand and one under each arm. I carried so many satchels that all you could see were satchels. You couldn't see no Leroy Paige."

By then your baggage will have acquired its own momentum, and you won't be able to exert much influence over it; so you can relax, and remember these pointers:

- When in a hurry to check out of a hotel, just pack everything that will fit into your bag or bags, and wear what's left over. If three shoes are left over, leave one as a tip.
- If your bag has a waterproof compartment for wet things, that is a good place to stow anything that doesn't have spaghetti sauce on it yet.
- If, when you shove your carry-on bag under the seat in front of you, the passenger in that seat jumps straight up into the air, this may be a sign that you will have some trouble getting the bag out again. Politely introduce yourself to the passenger in question, and ask if he or she would mind your pressing downward on his or her head and shoulders in order to flatten out any bag protuberances.
- Don't let your cat wear anything identifying him as your cat. He will be perfectly okay hanging around your hometown airport, with all the other inadvertently packed cats, until you get back. If your name is on him, however, you may be required to repack him and take him with you wherever you go. And many airlines do not allow bags containing cats to be stowed in overhead compartments.
- Should you wind up with someone else's bag by mistake, take the following quiz:
  1. I am traveling to
     a. Palm Springs
     b. Tokyo
     c. Worcester
  2. I have been on the road
     a. one day
     b. two days
     c. two weeks
  3. I am a
     a. cocaine dealer
     b. chief executive officer
     c. serious writer

4. I am taking this quiz with a
   a. gold pen
   b. gold pencil
   c. ballpoint that says PEEGEE'S PARTS, SPOKANE
5. I am traveling from
   a. Acapulco
   b. Palm Beach
   c. Amarillo

If the answers are c, c, c, c, and c, and you want to get ahead in the Reagan era, keep the other person's bag.

If Sheepskin, So Can You

(Some Friendly Remarks to Graduates)

I KNOW you young people are asking, "Will I be able to make it as a yuppie in the real world?"

Fortunately, most of you have had the foresight to equip yourselves with Greek. The real world is *basics*. In the real world the key thing is to get off a Greek allusion at the right moment.

Your department head buzzes you:

"Why the bejabbers haven't you pulled together that report on the substantiational aspects of that widget?"

You know what widget he means. The widget that your firm's new slickware floppy, the QUASI-2000, enables customers to visualize, in high-definitional three-dimensionality, on their cozily greenish screen.

"On the one hand . . . ," you reply, as you used to reply in seminars on Roots of the Renaissance to buy time. But time does not come so cheap in the real world. The intercom crackles. "I want to see *both* your hands on deck in about half a New York minute," snaps your crusty superior.

On your way to his module you pass the break area for employees who did not attend college. They are eating crude pastries from a machine and saying, "When you think of how bowling's changed in the last . . . it'll scare you." It is the job of a friend of yours in Human Resources to interface with these employees. "Don't ask," he has said.

With a smile virtually indistinguishable from the smile on your ID badge, you pass security and enter the highest corridor you are cleared for. There are no windows here, and the ducts are veiled by heavy mesh, but the air is ionized, so as to make you feel *coiled* as you never felt in halls of ivy. You enter the boss's module through his portico — an effect created by photographic enhancement, as he is only upper-middle management, but imposing just the same. His administrative assistant, Lavonna or Jeff, moves noiselessly, sinuously, into an alcove, where she or he takes care of certain nuts and bolts.

"For corn sakes-a-jumpin'-mighty!" expostulates the Old Man, who is staring moodily at his screen, presumably at the widget in question. (He always keeps his office console situated so that only he can see the screen.) "We know it's highly defined. We know it's three-dimensional. We know we can cathodically cause it to rotate through three hundred sixty degrees on any of its five construable axes, or to go inside out and back again and inside out and back again and inside out and back again, *foop* f'lup, *foop* f'lup, *foop* f'lup. But what *is* it? It looks like a, oh, what am I thinking of? A . . ." For the first time he cuts his eyes at you.

"Self-slicing zucchini?" you hazard.

"No! That's not what I was thinking of *at all!*" the boss exclaims. He dashes a mugful of Hearty Fella Mock Cheese Soup across your shirtfront and ID badge. This is one way in which the real world differs from academe. Professors did not throw soup on you for wrong answers. Because your salary did not come through them. The situation was almost vice versa, in fact. Sure, your professors had their own research deal with the American Better Lipids Council. ("There Are Lipids, and Then There Are Lipids.") But if your parents had not been ponying up $14,000 a year for your education, then your professors would have had to be directly employed by the ABLC, on a salaried rather than a funded basis, and would have lost their independence. ABLC department heads would have been throwing soup — and fatty soup, frankly — on them. So your professors took a professorial, which is to say a crypto-truckling, tone with you.

Not so in the real world. Here it is all what-are-you-packing and hey-nonny-nonny. Your boss can roll you up in a strip of carpet and whale the living daylights out of you with a length of technological cable if he so elects. He is interested in one thing — performance and performance only.

Because, remember: his department has to perform if he is to get the bonus that will enable him to pony up $14,000 a year for each of his offspring to attend college for five, six, seven years. (Today's offspring take longer and longer to emerge into the real world.) If in order to get performance out of you he has to be a hard guy occasionally, then so be it. Furthermore, in the real world bosses must finally come to terms with the fact that they enjoy whaling the daylights out of people less highly placed than themselves.

But Greek resounds across the ages. Presumably you have been an officer in your sorority or fraternity, and therefore are privy to classical rites. And you have read the rushing narratives of Xenophon in the original — probably staying up all night the night before the exam, pizza and No-Doz and the ancient texts, you can't tell me anything, I've been there.

Okay. You've got your good grounding in Greek. Use it.

It is a mistake to venture a guess about what the boss has in mind as to what the widget actually is. If the boss actually has anything in mind, it is beside the point. *Process* is the point. Go with your Greek.

"Τί ἠμπορεῖς νὰ καμνης μετὰ χέρια σου [What can you do with your hands]?" you say.

Your boss concedes you a small smile.

" Ἠμπορῶ νὰ ἐργάζωμαι μετὰ χέρια μου [I can work with my hands]," he says.

"Τί ἠμπορεῖς νὰ κάμνης μετὰ πόδια σου [What can you do with your feet]?" you go on.

His smile grows somewhat larger. " Ἠμπορῶ νὰ περιπατῶ μετὰ πόδια μου. [I can walk with my feet]," he replies. "Now one for you: Τί κάμνεις μὲ την μύτην σου [What do you do with your nose]?"

You are ready. "Μυρίζω μὲ τὴν μύτην μου [I smell with my nose]" is your reponse.

" Ἠμπορεῖς νὰ ἰδῆς μὲ τὴν μύτην σου [Can you see with your nose]?"

" Ὄχι. Δέν ἠμπορῶ νὰ ἰδῶ μὲ τὴν μύτην μου. Βλέπω μὲ τὰ μάτια μου. Ἀκούω μὲ αὐτιά μου. Μασσῶ μὲ τὰ δόντια μου [No. I cannot see with my nose. I see with my eyes. I hear with my ears. I chew with my teeth]."

And then the boss joins you in unison: "Πηγαίνω ἐδῶ καὶ ἐκεῖ μὲ τὰ πόδια μου [I go here and there with my feet]."

But the boss has not lost sight of the bottom line. "How about the widget?" he says.

"Syzygy," you say then. A term derived from Greek. You don't know what it means. Remember: you can never appear to be cleverer than you are if you never fake anything.

"Eh?" says the boss. "Hmm . . . Syz . . . Hm." He doesn't know what it means either.

But he has not gotten where he is without acquiring certain resources. He flutters his keyboard, as if manipulating the widget. What he is actually doing is punching up his vocabulary — 400,000 words phonetically arranged.

Now his look is sly: "I kinda have a notion," he says, "that you don't have in mind *syzygy* in the astronomical sense: the nearly straight-line configuration of three celestial bodies in a gravitational system." He winks. "No sir, I kinda think you have in mind the prosodical sense: a group of two coupled feet."

You don't say anything.

Now he presumably does have the widget on his screen. *Foop* f'lup, *foop* f'lup. "Group of two coupled feet, huh? It might be. By granny" — he slaps his desk resoundingly, manually — "it *looks* like feet. Lavonna [or Jeff]! More soup!"

The boss regards you with a new mellowness. Leans back in his chair and cups his belly: "Hm! You know what the fella says: 'I used to look like a Greek god. Now I look like a g.d. Greek!' " Your boss laughs and laughs, till he is fit to be tied.

So you tie him, with a length of technological cable, and stash him in the utility cubicle. By the time Lavonna or Jeff returns (in college you will not have known anyone like Lavonna or Jeff, who is not into mind trips, who is into taking care of certain nuts and bolts, who asks nothing more in return than to marry you resentfully and give you offspring, rarer than days in June, whom you will be putting through college for the rest of your life), you are ready for the soup.

How to Raise Your Boy to Play Pro Ball

SINCE I have done a good deal of work in the sportswriting field, people ask me, "Where did you get that unusual tan?" (I go to a nearby tannery every spring, lay out twenty-eight dollars and a little something for the attendant, and have myself dipped.) "What is the right grip for squash?" (Grasp the squash firmly by the neck with your left hand, then take a knife with the right hand and bring it down in short, crisp strokes on the part of the squash not covered by the left hand.) But most of all they ask me, "How do I raise my boy to be a professional football player?" This last question I answer by saying, "Set an example. Lay and finish nine sets of steps in one day."

And then I speak of concrete grit, pride of workmanship, and what Ray Mansfield's father, the man who laid the steps, called "that preservation meanness."

Mansfield still sells his millions of insurance in Pittsburgh, but he has finished out his career on the gridiron, where, he once told me, he felt like a knight in armor. For over a decade, through 1976, he was the Steelers' starting center, emergency placekicker, and stalwart of beer and stories. The Old Ranger, they called him. Still call him, actually. His father, Owen Mansfield, was proof that you can be legendary in your work even if your work isn't something glamorous like bowling people over so that somebody can run a leather-covered bladder past them.

In '75 I went with Ray to visit Owen in Kennewick, Washington. Owen was a tall, well-preserved-looking man of sixty-five who had finally given up heavy labor because of his heart. He puttered around his small house, picked and sang Jimmie Rodgers songs, and reminisced about working and fighting.

Owen grew up on an Arkansas farm. When he was no more than a sprout himself, he was "putting sprouts in the new ground. Start plowing and the plow would hit me in the stomach. Plow'd run into a root right under the ground, the mules would stop, the end of the plow would come around and hit me in the shin." But he had the example of *his* father before him. "My dad. That was the workingest old man you ever saw. And he was a Christian, believed in living right. I remember one day my dad was getting the best of Uncle Port, and Uncle Port's dog run up and bit him. He turned around and held Uncle Port and hollered, 'Somebody kill that god-d . . . that dog.' He thought better of himself, you see. Uncle Port was the meanest man that ever hit that country down there."

Since he couldn't be the meanest or the most industrious man in Arkansas, in the late twenties Owen rode the rails west. He'd stop off and scratch around for work or live off the land. "I remember if somebody had eaten a lot of bananas, I'd pick up them banana peelings and eat 'em. They was good. I could eat a tree, I believe." He dodged the railroad cops. "Texas Slim. He lined up forty of us one time and said, 'All right. First one that catches the train, I'm going to shoot him.' He wore a nice suit, a big white hat, two guns. He was a *nice*-looking guy. But a *mean* son of a gun. I just patted my hands when I heard he was killed. I wish I'd a been a fast draw, *I*'d a killed him.

"I was 'Slim,' too, all my life nearly, working. Had the longest neck of anybody in the country."

His first job as a married man was splitting logs for rails.

33

He and Mrs. Mansfield eventually had nine kids. When Ray was born, the family was living in a tent in a farm labor camp outside Bakersfield, California, and Owen was in the hospital with a rattlesnake bite. "They gave me a shot of some stuff and I started trembling all over, got quivery all through my body. I said, 'Dag burn it, I guess I'm going to die in this little old place.'

"Then, when I got well, our first daughter, Merelene, got pneumonia. They took Merelene to the same room I'd been in. Wasn't long till she died. I tell you, it was hard times. She was seven and a half. Merelene. A name I studied out myself, to get something there wasn't anything like."

"We all took Merelene back to Missouri," Ray says. "Like the marines never leave their dead behind, my parents didn't want to leave their child out there in California on the road. This was in 'forty-one. Dad put Merelene and all the rest of us except Gene, my oldest brother, on the train, and then he put a mattress on the back seat of the car and put Gene on it and just took off. I don't know whether he got to Missouri before the train or just after it. Driving a broken-down 1929 Chevy. Mother said she saw my dad the whole day, off and on, when the road came close to the tracks."

Owen told me, "The car broke down once and I was fixing it and that train passed. Made me so lonesome I couldn't sit still."

When they got Merelene buried back home, they headed back out looking for a place to settle. A few years later, living in Arizona, Owen flipped a coin to decide whether to go just to Joplin, Missouri, or all the way to the state of Washington. And Washington won. That's where Ray grew up, in Kennewick, where Owen got into concrete. "One of the hardest jobs in America," Ray says.

"Dad was always top hand on the job," says Ray's younger brother Bill, who played football at Washington State and now is back in Kennewick, in concrete himself. "It's a good thing he's not working today. It'd kill him to see the way people work these days. He wasn't any college professor, but he was as good as there was at what he did. Guys like him are gone forever. We'd lay a floor, I'd think it was finished — it would be, today — and he'd say, 'Son, we can't leave until you can dance on it.'

"You talk to Dad's old foreman and he says, 'That Owen was the finest-working man I ever knew.' When we'd work with him, he'd grab a shovel and all you'd see was sand. A forty-eight-year-old man outworking our ass. When he was fifty-nine years old, he was going full speed. My brother Gene kept saying, 'Dad, cool it a little bit.' He'd say, 'Ah, let's get the job done.' Now it's: make money and get by if you can. He never learned. . . ."

Ray says, "We grew up expecting to work. It came with breathing air. He hired us out when I was in the second or third grade. Me and my sister and older brother, we'd be out at four in the morning cutting asparagus until eight, go right from work to school.

"When I got older, I'd sell papers on the streets. I just loved being on the streets. Even though there wasn't but one main street in Kennewick. I was afraid I would miss something.

"I worked all one morning to get fifteen cents to go to the movie. I ran all the way to the movie and found out it was twenty cents. I ran all the way home, pissed off, kicking things. I told my father what was wrong. (He was home in between his work in concrete. He had to lay it in the morning, wait for it to set, and then go back late to finish it up.) He reached in his pocket, pulled out a handful of sand, and came up with a nickel. His fingers all dry and split open from the concrete. He gave me the nickel. It was probably the only nickel in the house. I ran all the way back to the movie: James Mason as Rommel in *The Desert Fox.*

"When I came home, my father was back at work. I lay awake until one in the morning, when he came home. I sneaked downstairs and watched him get undressed and go to bed. I never thanked him. I just wanted to look at him and think what kind of dad I had.

"There was so much warmth around the house," Ray says. "We didn't have any mean kids in our family. Everybody was loving of each other and tolerant of other people. I got into a lot of fights, but I didn't like it especially. If you ever want to get a Mansfield mad, pick on another Mansfield. We've got almost too much family pride. I remember there was a big kid around Campbell's Cabins, where we lived for a while. I did everything I could to avoid him. But he picked on my little brother Odie, and I went after him and nearly coldcocked him. I had no fear when one of my brothers was being picked on. But even after I whipped that big kid, I was still scared of him."

Bill tells an old family story: "This guy, thirty-five, got into an altercation with our grandfather, Pa, when Pa was sixty-five years old. Our Uncle Granville was seventeen, and he goes flying through the air, kicks the guy's ass through the dusty streets till the guy whimpers like a dog and gets out of there. My dad's eyes gleam when he tells about it. That's why it was good having Moynihan in the U.N. You can't take too much shit."

Ray and Bill Mansfield and I were drinking and getting profound in this place in Kennewick, and Bill said to Ray, "Remember when we were working out — I was just getting ready to go to Washington State — and you said, 'Bill, don't ever, ever accept getting beat. Don't ever let a guy beat you and walk away and say, "Well, he beat me." You have to fight and scratch and bite. If you're bleeding and crying and scratching and shitting, keep on fighting and that guy will quit. As long as *you* don't.' "

Not many occupations today bring together fighting and working the way football does. But working was a kind of fighting for Owen. And both working and fighting were kinds of sports. "I'd get a kick out of troweling cement with other trowelers," he said. "Out of staying about the length of this table ahead of the other fella. That would tickle me to death." The story about their father that made Ray's and Bill's eyes light up the brightest — Bill almost boiled up out of his chair telling it — was the one about the steps.

"He laid and finished *nine sets of steps in one day*. Did a Cool Hand Luke shot. Then two thousand, three thousand square feet of concrete. It was superhuman. How it happened: It was a Monday, and the man told him it had to be done by Wednesday. My dad said, 'Don't worry.' The man said, 'Well, you better get it done.'

"That made my dad mad. So he said, 'I'll show you.' And he did it all in eight hours. Edged it, everything. He was running the whole time, and he was forty-five. When he finished, there was smoke coming off his body, but there were the nine sets of steps. All those assholes were scratching their heads and saying, How did he do it? It's still a legend around here."

Right after Ray's last season, Owen was talking to Gene and Odie, and they told him he'd better do something about his hair — he'd let it grow awfully long. "I'm not going to get a haircut," Owen said. "I'm going to go buy a dress." And he rocked back laughing and suddenly died.

Afterward, Ray's brother told him Owen had been glad that Ray was retiring from football. Owen had said he'd always thought of Ray as a boy, of course, but that Ray was getting too old to play a kid's game.

How May Human Chimneys and Fresh-Air Fiends Share the Same World?

To confirmed smokers, smoke is a balm. To devout non-smokers, it is an abomination. Just what we need: another religious war.

Cigarette smoking, I am smugly pleased to say, is one of the few halfway legal things that have never caught my fancy. I can enjoy a joint or a good cigar if someone hands me one (aren't you glad people don't pass the latter around the way they do the former?), and when I was younger I smoked a pipe often enough that I gave some thought to developing the knack of gesturing, in conversation, with the stem. Then one day I bade an expansive "Hey there!" to someone I knew, forgetting that my pipe was in my mouth, and the whole thing — stem, bowl, ashes, embers, and dottle — dropped into my lap. And I said to myself at the time, "Well, if you do this sort of thing very often, people may begin to think you are not a serious person."

I have never understood why so many people object more strenuously to cigar and pipe smoke than they do to, say, Merit vapors. A nice fresh dollar panatela or a brier packed with Virginia-and-latakia mixture smells like something flavorful cooking; filter cigarettes just smell like something thin burning.

So I do not enjoy sitting next to some heathen (by "heathen" I mean someone who pisses me off) who holds a fumy Winston in just such a way as to snake a carcinogenic tendril directly into my nose.

On the other hand, since I have never been able to stop doing anything that *does* catch my fancy, I feel a certain solidarity with tobacco addicts — some of whom, indeed, are my companions in other health-threatening pursuits, like talking at great length loudly until long after we have run out of ice. If I like somebody, and the room isn't too small, I don't mind their smoke any more than I really mind the fact that my dogs fart. I mean it registers on me occasionally, but I don't dwell on it. And philosophically, although nothing constricts my breathing like the proximity of a libertarian in full espousal, I take a generally antiprohibitionist stance.

However. Only the Shadow knows how many cancer-encouraging, heart-discouraging influences lurk in even a clean-living modern American's system. A person I met recently who was in chemical research told me that *plastic* — for instance, refrigerator-storage wraps and bags — exudes carcinogenic molecules. I don't see how I could live without plastic. Strangers' cigarette smoke, though, I don't need.

So it is good that movie sweethearts rarely light up anymore. (Instead, they simulate oral sex.) It is good that more people notice that smoke bothers them. (I must say it never struck me as a clear violation of my personal space until recent years, but then neither did Republicanism.) If there were a nicotine head in my household, I might well remind that loved one occasionally, with tact ("Do you think there'll be ashtrays in Heaven?"), of studies that find a high cancer rate among nonsmokers living with smokers. I have one new measure to propose:

Waiting areas — in airports, hospitals, bus stations, Limbo — should be divided into smoking and nonsmoking sections. Waiting in designated areas is, if not carcinogenic in itself, so dismal that it stimulates the smoking urge and also the outrage reflex. Puffers and huffers should be kept apart.

But banning all smoking on airplanes and in other places where nicotinists must fidget for long periods of time is too much like flogging. People who smoke writhe like salted caterpillars when they can't. It is not excruciatingly difficult, most of the time, for nonsmokers to circulate through contemporary life without becoming trapped in the lesser distress that smoke-inhalation causes them.

Far more obnoxious than smokers, to me, are people who seem to relish the opportunity to upbraid smokers for perceived foulness. I know lovely people who smoke; I once knew (not for long) a woman who found it refreshing to jog through the fumes of Central Park but would snarl "That's a filthy habit" at people who smoked near her and, if they didn't desist immediately, would actually snatch the smoking materials out of their mouths. It would not break my heart to hear that she had been run over by a truck full of Lucky Strikes.

According to a cover story in *Time,* a revival of manners is under way. I would like to see manners flourish between smokers and nonsmokers.

Let us go to one of those waiting areas I was talking about. In an airport. Any traveler knows that hell is other passengers. Especially when nothing is moving except passengers' twitches.

A man is sitting next to a woman with a small child who is running in tiny circles and then falling flat, rooting on the floor for a while, and then getting up to run in tiny circles some more — all the time engaging in an unengaging form of wordplay: "Blinkle blinkle blittle blar, blow I blunder blut you blare."

"Mind if I smoke?" asks the man.

"Oh, I'm sorry, but I'm actually allergic to smoke," says the woman civilly. "I suppose I could go over by the window."

The man does not say he is allergic to the woman's small child. He says, "Wouldn't hear of it. *I'll* go over by the window."

Actually, of course, there is no openable window in the airport. But neither party acknowledges this fact, lest they begin to scream.

"Well," says the woman, "I hate to inconvenience you. As a matter of fact little Janie and I need to stretch our legs, don't we Janie?"

"Bletch our blegs, bletch our blegs."

"Tell you what. I'll have a smoke while you're gone and when you get back I'll teach little Janie how to whistle."

Is that so hard? Okay, okay. Is it impossible?

What if *graciousness* became a widespread habit? It would offset a lot of smoke in the atmosphere. There are more powerful carcinogens around than cigarette smoke, and self-righteousness may well be one of them.

Then too, umbrage is as fierce an addiction as smoking. So let me address the user and the bluenose who get wind of each other:

Eschew tense snappiness, which is bad for the blood pressure. Welcome the chance to blow off steam, not snidely but with eloquence and gesticulation. Hand-waving and a brisk flow of words help clear the air. They also provide some of the satisfactions of smoking. And you never know when Ted Koppel will happen by and invite you both to go on "Nightline."

Can Brunswick Stew Be Upscaled?

I AM the first to admit that Brunswick stew, which I think the world of, lacks the mystique of chili. I don't admit for one minute that the Southwest has any notion of real barbecue, but I will admit freely that those folks out there have generated more mystique around their chili than Southeasterners like me have around Brunswick stew.

You never read about Brunswick stew-offs, where people compete to put the finest, hottest, most natural, and hairiest (figuratively speaking) ingredients together into the most definitive bowl of mushy, tangy, reddish-brown-with-yaller-specks stuff.

This is partly because, what kind of hat would you wear to a Brunswick stew-off? And partly because Brunswick Stewoff sounds like the son of an Anglophiliac movie agent.

"Chili" is a sexier term than "Brunswick stew." If you doubt it, try saying "chili-chili-chili-chili-*hoo*-pah!" in a bouncy, finger-popping kind of tone and then try the same thing with "Brunswick-stew-Brunswick-stew-ick . . ." I don't think you will get as far as the *hoo*-pah. No one enjoys setting out toward a *hoo*-pah and bogging down.

On the other hand a long slow rolling "Bruuuuuu*uhn*-z-wick stoooo" has resonance. So if the Brunswick stew industry (should there be one) were to hire the right public-relations firm, and change the name slightly so that someone could throw in a lot of extra hot sauce and market Third-Degree *Burns*wick Stew, it would probably become commonplace within the next few years to find out that your daughter is rooming with a former stew princess at some fancy college.

But I would hate to see Brunswick stew blown out of proportion. I think that's what has happened to chili, frankly. Chili to me is like peaches: even out of a can it's not bad. In fact that's the only way I ever had it until I was twenty-three years old. That's why you have to make a mystique of chili, to justify not eating it out of a can.

Whereas Brunswick stew isn't put out by Hormel; it just crops up, at barbecues and in barbecue places. No one knows what is in it. It may be a by-product of the hickory-smoking process — resulting when small animals running somewhere with ears of corn in their mouths tumble into the open pit.

And sometimes it's not good. Sometimes. I will urge some people who have never had Brunswick stew (nobody but a Russian has never had chili) to try it, and I'll tell them it's named for General Lionel Brunswick, who discovered that you can mix anything with okra, and I'll assure them that boy, do they have a treat in store for them. And then it will arrive and it won't be good, sometimes.

That's why I'm glad Brunswick stew doesn't have the mystique that chili has. Anybody who has ever glanced at an in-flight magazine knows what goes into authentic chili: antelope chunks, hand-chewed Guatemalan cumin, individually seeded and dried chili peppers (only the ones that point upward on the bush) from the Aiyaiyai region of Oaxaca, and no beans, because chili in a can has beans. But no one, even the Brunswick family, can say for sure what goes into Brunswick stew, or what doesn't.

Which means that I can be authoritative about it. When people complain that this Brunswick stew I have touted them onto is not good, I can roll a bite of it around against my upper palate, gaze off into the middle distance with my eyes closed except for tiny contemplative slits, and observe, with no tinge of defensiveness, "Yeah, this is a little off. Prob'ly used a rabid squirrel."

How to Read the *New York Times*

THE first thing I look for is whether I am in it. Many mornings — the majority of mornings — I am not. This fuels my belief that the *Times* has me black- or at least brown-listed. Every writer who is neither rich nor a member of the American Academy of Arts and Letters has a right to this belief. William Styron is in the *Times* nearly every morning, being either reviewed or quoted. Sure! He probably goes skiing with those guys!

The second thing I look for in the *Times* is something juicy. This may seem quixotic. I realize that the *Times* gives the impression that it doesn't want to admit that there actually is anything in the world that Weegee would have liked to photograph. But when there does occur a murder or an accidental squashing that the newspaper of record cannot in all good conscience overlook, the *Times* always comes up with good obscure details. Several years ago the *Times* ran a story about a helicopter crash that killed twenty-one people being transported to Disneyland. A witness was quoted as saying, "Two small gears and a dime hit me on the chest."

I don't mean to outrage traditionalists, but I recommend looking in the *Times* for signs of writing that is not wholly institutional. It's there. It's like little rustles of life in the forest primeval: it's there if you look for it.

But don't tell anybody.

Living with Wizardry

I WAS talking to a grade-school teacher the other day. She said some of her students were wholly nonplussed by the concept of clockwise, and she had figured out why: all the timepieces they had been exposed to were digital.

What is Western culture going to do without the concept of clockwise? How are newspapers going to identify people in group photographs?

> The one just to the left of the water pitcher there is Prime Minister Margaret Thatcher. The one to her left — not to your, the reader's, left, which is to say what has just been referred to as "the" left, but rather to her (Mrs. Thatcher's) left — is Earvin "Magic" Johnson. Okay, now, keep moving in that direction in an orbital manner, so to speak. Pretend you are revolving around the ice sculpture there, and . . .

Whatever else may be miniaturized in the years ahead, it won't be photo captions.

But I haven't got time to worry about the impact of electronic wizardry on newspapers. I am too busy worrying about the impact of it on me.

In my own home.

There is a word processor in my home.

"Word processor," indeed! That thing doesn't know what

words are. A word, to that thing, is whatever comes between spaces. That thing would just as soon process *tbldgk* as it would *mellifluous.* Unless it has some kind of correct-spelling program in it, in which case it would probably refuse to process *tbldgk* on the grounds that there is no such entity that fits between spaces. So you see, this essay could not have been written on that thing.

But I realize that is not your, the reader's, problem. So let me ask you this. You have a VCR in your home? You have any children in your home that drink Kool-Aid?

In our case, by all firsthand accounts, no particular child was involved. It was one of those spontaneous Kool-Aid spills that happen. But only children were present. It cost $270 to fix.

One jelly glass of Kool-Aid tips itself over into the VCR, and there goes $270. You know why? Because when it comes to these electronic things, there are too many angels in there dancing on the head of a pin. If man had been meant to compress so many angels that he could drown $270 worth of them with one glass of Kool-Aid, he would have been given children who might be pinned down and held liable for such sums.

Had the VCR been a Stradivarius, the Kool-Aid could have been wiped off with a sponge. If it had been my Royal standard manual typewriter, bought used nineteen years ago, nobody would ever have noticed. You'd have to spill a pot of chili into my typewriter to make it operate any worse than it does already. Can you imagine what it probably costs to spill a *spoonful* of chili into a word processor? I don't even want to think about it. Forget I mentioned it. And I like to eat while I'm working.

My wife, Joan Ackermann-Blount, and I both write. At home. A cottage industry. Our 115-year-old house in the Berkshires used to be a parsonage. It had too many angels dancing in it already, before electronic wizardry started crowding in. But I had some faint idea of how to deal with those angels. I could imagine why the house creaked where it creaked (someday, unless I am just saying this, I intend to shim up the old floorboards), and why it leaked where it leaked (because New England pipes get a kick out of freezing when they are owned by someone from Georgia), and what made that skittering sound within the walls (an escaped hamster named Sherry, or her ghost).

The more electronic our home becomes, however, the more it becomes the department of the electronicians. If an electronician tells me it costs, say, $1,140 to fix a word processor that has had Kool-Aid spilled into it, how am I going to argue? It's like being kidnapped by savages and told I'm going to have to paint my head blue. What am I going to say? "That doesn't sound right to me"?

I'll tell you what doesn't sound right to me. That word processor we've got now. When you type on it you have to be gentle, and it makes a little twiddly noise. (I don't want to twiddle out a story, I want to bang one out. I want to be saying to my typewriter, "Take that! Take that!" Because I know my typewriter is going to be saying back, "Yeah, right.") And when the printer prints, it makes the sound of someone doggedly running a fingernail back and forth over the teeth of a comb.

So how did it get into our house?

Well, I'll admit, I have gone back and forth on this word processor question. For years I said, firmly, "Nope. Not me. Just give me a stub pencil, an eyeshade, and a wet whistle, and I can turn out as much copy as anybody else can on one of these futuristic deals that require eighty books of instructions and a backup generator."

People would say, "I actually find I write better on a word processor." I'd say, "Uh-huh. Isn't it a shame Flaubert didn't have one?"

But then all the newspapers in the land and half my friends converted, and I started saying, "Well, I guess it's coming. We might as well face it. We are all going to be using one of those gadgets someday."

Then someone said, "Yep. They say it more closely approximates the workings of the human mind."

And it occurred to me: who wants to approximate — if mine is any example — the workings of the human mind? I know my typewriter doesn't want to. The great thing about my typewriter is its native toughness. Every couple of years it seems to be getting crankier than usual, but then a bent screw falls out of its insides and it settles back down. None of these screws has had to be replaced. In four places, my typewriter is held together with duct tape. My typewriter is from the old school, and doesn't want to wade through a lot of fancy convolutions. My typewriter is always saying to my mind, "Hey, let's tighten this up."

So the next time somebody said, "I actually find I write better on a word processor," I said, "Uh-huh. That's what they used to say about drugs."

But then the whole question of storage and retrieval came up. It was explained to me that you could pump cratefuls of information into a word processor, and those angels would tamp it all down into a little disk, and when you wanted any of it back you just pushed a button and those angels would find it for you.

That is something my typewriter will not do. My typewriter sits in the midst of stacks and clumps and windrows of information-filled paper. If I were to ask my typewriter to retrieve something from all this mess, it would look at me as if I were out of my human mind. I can usually find what I am looking for, myself, but when I come up with it I feel like I have finally caught a rabbit after chasing it through flocks and flocks of chickens.

And there are feathers all over the house. My store of information threatens to overwhelm, without in the least enlightening, the household. I have files that creak louder than the floorboards do, folders that shed worse than the cats. Sometimes I feel bad about this.

So when Joan — who hates a digital clock because it

doesn't have a face — and my son John — who won't even use an aluminum bat — started saying we ought to get a word processor, I thought, well, no cottage industry can afford to drag its feet. And it's hard not to drag them when there are papers up to your ankles. Maybe we ought to modernize, I thought.

Then we talked price. And I started yelling, "No! No! It's right here in the Bill of Rights somewhere, that no citizen shall be required to lay out two thousand dollars in order to express himself! And what happens when people start splashing Kool-Aid around?"

So Joan bought a word processor on her own.

That's why we have it in our house.

And a script I wrote is filed away in it. Because that way, when I have to make revisions, I don't have to re-bang out the entire thing. I can just twiddle in the revisions and, presto, let the printer plickplickplick out a new whole.

Only the revised script is due now. And there is something wrong with the printer. Its old ribbon is exhausted, after one run-through, and it refuses to accept a new one. (My typewriter doesn't give up on a ribbon until it has been reduced to ribbons.) So what am I supposed to do? Take a series of photographs of the script as it appears in segments on the word processor's screen, and mail those in? The electronicians have been summoned.

As I await these divines, I am feeling less guilty about my mess of papers. One thing about my mess of papers, I can always get my hands on it. In fact I have to dig out from under it every time I get up from my typewriter.

And I am always finding things I never knew I had. For instance, I just found a copy of the *Times* from December 7, 1968, which I saved because my son was born the day before. And look what else was happening that day:

PUBLIC TO TAPE-RECORD IDEAS FOR NIXON

White Plains, Dec. 6 — Aides to Richard Nixon are planning to try out electronic listening posts in Westchester

County and Alabama later this month as a means to let the President-elect hear from "the forgotten American."

A spokesman at Mr. Nixon's New York office said today the pilot projects were designed to test "a means of finding out what people are thinking and what the issues and problems are."

Volunteers for the project in this suburban county . . . said they were planning to take tape machines into schools, colleges, town meetings and rich and poor neighborhoods to record the attitudes of people who want to reach their Government. . . .

What if Nixon had stuck with this program, and expanded it to the point where he was tape-recording everybody in the nation *except* himself? What if our government had placed a tape recorder in every American home?

I think I am going to go mix up a pitcher of Kool-Aid.

Men, Women, and Projectiles

Salute to John Wayne

A FEW years ago, before nakedness became old hat, I was
standing near Times Square looking at an opaque
storefront behind which, according to a boldly lettered sign,
you could talk to a nude woman. It wasn't the kind of thing I
would do, but I stood there wondering what it would be like,
what I would say to her, whether she would feel obliged to
respond.

As I began to move on, I found myself surrounded by
green arms: an army colonel and a staff sergeant materialized, passed each other and me at the same time, and exchanged crisp salutes.

Although these two may have been the only servicemen in
the entire midtown area, their eyes did not meet. You can
tell by looking at a person's eyes whether they are meeting
someone else's. Both men were in fact angling their attention
toward the TALK TO A NUDE WOMAN sign, but at any rate
each of them addressed himself, quite properly, to the uniform, not the man.

I sensed an epiphany, or at least a *déjà vu*. Except that
there seemed to be an element missing. I turned back to the
storefront. What if the woman were actually quite good
company: hearty, secure, at peace, her skin tautly billowy
like a flag?

Still, you might be at some pains to give her the impression that so far as you were concerned, she was not the only fish in the sea. And she might want to convey that although you might be with a large accounting firm, and her own occupation was being talked to nude, she was not your bit of fluff.

It hit me. What was missing.

Then she came out, slightly but not unfetchingly cross-eyed, and wearing — something loose. I can never, except where they are revealing, describe women's clothes. But hers reminded me of the time in seventh grade when I showed up at my girlfriend Amy's house unexpectedly the afternoon before a Methodist hayride I was taking her to and she seemed more domestic than she did at school. She smelled of hand lotion, something I did not understand the appeal of. Her hair was wet, and she was wearing the kind of flapabout clothes one's mother wore while giving herself a home permanent. Then, through fabric, I descried the unsegmented line of Amy's whole flank. I didn't recall having seen that line, moving and unbroken by band or ruffle, before.

Amy, flustered, offered me a Coke. While she was getting it, I sat down. Her orange-and-white cat jumped into my lap and started kneading my crotch in an embarrassing way. I half stood, but the cat clung. I pulled at the cat, the cat sank its claws into me, and I was hopping, hunched, trying to wrangle the cat loose, when Amy came in with my Coke.

"Mister Fluff!" she cried, and her eyes filled with tears.

Well, that was the element. When this nude woman in mufti came out of the storefront, she was carrying a plush but alert-looking gray cat. You know how hard it is to pin down a cat's focus, but this one gave me a look, I thought, as his mistress went pitter-pat on high heels right by me, sprang into a taxi, and was gone.

Did she hold the cat, stroking it, in her lap or at her bosom, as she was being talked to? Did she let visitors touch it? Certain visitors? When I am trying to concentrate on

56

something, cats drive me crazy, and yet I am drawn to them. To pet the cat of a not unfetching woman who is tangibly unavailable, as she watches, I imagine would be exciting but not salutary.

Associations were gathering quickly now. The salutes by which I had just been bracketed were the first I had seen in some time. They took me back to the mid-sixties, when nudity and antimilitarism were growing rampant among the young, and I was a callow, married army lieutenant. Other twenty-three-year-old Americans were daubing "Peace" and "Love" on their foreheads and filling the picture magazines with Human Be-Ins. I had grown up imprinted with sentiments like "Do your bit" and "If you must talk to a nude woman, start a family."

What adults did, I had gathered, was marry, for life; Paul had told the Corinthians that it was better to marry than to burn. I had been burning since the seventh grade. So I married. And suddenly the conscience of America was single, anti-grown-up, and running around naked at Make Love Not War rallies.

These youths must have come along a few years too late to be affected, as I had been in 1949 at the age of eight, by *The Sands of Iwo Jima,* in which John Wayne plays a sergeant who turns raw recruits into fighting men. Since I was palpably raw, and I loved playing gun battle, and John Wayne was John Wayne, that movie struck me with the force of an imperative.

Looking at it today, you might think that *The Sands of Iwo Jima* would put a decent-minded boy off warfare, since it features the broiling of what John Wayne calls "little lemon-colored characters" in pillboxes. But you don't have the feeling that John Wayne enjoys that kind of thing. The movie's great theme is the difficulty of getting through to people.

Wayne keeps trying to strike a rapport with John Agar, who plays a raw recruit whose father, a legendary colonel, was killed in action. Wayne's own son (from whom he is now estranged) is named after Agar's father, under whom Wayne once served. Agar, for his part, is bitter toward his father, who regarded Agar as "too soft." At mail call Agar learns of the birth of *his* son. When Wayne tries to congratulate him, Agar tells Wayne, coldly, pointedly, "I won't insist that he read the Marine Corps manual. Instead I'll get him a set of Shakespeare."

Wayne's eyes narrow, but with feeling. "I've tried every approach to you that I know, and got nowhere," he tells Agar. Eventually the two of them become close, after Agar saves Wayne's life by dispatching an impending Asian with an entrenching tool. Agar says, "There's something I've been trying to say, but I just can't seem to find the words."

Wayne says, "You mean you been to two universities and still can't find the words to say you been out of line?"

Then we see Wayne get killed by a sniper, and the famous flag-raising scene. Inside Wayne's shirt Agar finds a letter to Wayne's son that says, "Always do what your heart tells you is right."

I don't say, even in retrospect, that this is bad advice. But it doesn't clear up the obliqueness in *The Sands of Iwo Jima,* which I never quite got out of my system. Furthermore, the notion that becoming a fighting man was profoundly connected with adulthood stuck with me, through two universities, all the way up until I entered the army. It was ROTC camp that took the pleasure out of weapons for me. To get our attention, one Korea-vet instructor went *fwooof* with a flamethrower and said, "Presto! Chinese hamburger!" By then I was already sworn in.

I embarked upon two years of bureaucratic lieutenancy. The Vietnam buildup began. I was unable to see the point of burning villages in order to save them. I *could* see a certain appeal, for a guy my age, in friendly nude anarchy. I was living in married-junior-officer quarters and exchanging salutes.

When saluted by young men who had the good taste to be not only disaffected soldiers, like me, but also uncommissioned, I felt what is known as role strain. And they knew it. Once I fell from a bicycle in front of a leaf-raking detail — three stockade prisoners whose sudden salute I tried to return while pedaling, balancing, and holding on to some papers. I and the papers fell into the leaves. The prisoners remained at attention. "Let's all desert!" I felt like saying, but I was in no position to.

What you were supposed to say when you ran into a knot of enlisted men who were engaged in the accomplishment of their mission was "Carry on." I didn't like the sound of it. Even when not climbing out of a pile of leaves, I tried to give "Carry on" a tongue-in-cheek twist, but then it seemed to imply too racy an authorization. What if some specialist 4, caught body-painting a general's daughter, were to exclaim, "But this lieutenant said I was to carry on"?

What really bothered me, though, was being saluted by a topkick or a sergeant major who looked as if he might have served with John Wayne at Iwo Jima. Clear as it was to me that the army at the upper levels did not know what it was doing, it was just as clear that this sergeant was my superior in years, training, job responsibility, and devotion to duty. He would signal himself officially beneath me with a salute snappy enough to cut ice, a salute that, however, leaned over backward not to contain any hint of "You mooncalf, sir." I tried to develop a *wry* return-of-salute, but that is difficult.

I was myself required, of course, to salute superior officers — not as an oppressed person, which would have fit my mood, but as an accomplice. Here I showed some sixties spirit. Once, I saluted a major who was using one hand to take a last drag on a cigarette and the other to hold his hat on against the wind. A colonel would just have nodded, but this major, a young one, lost his hat and bit through his cigarette. Even a full bird colonel could be made to feel overacknowledged, I found, if saluted from fifty yards away, or while he was playing golf, or while the saluter was having a tooth filled.

A general, on the other hand, could not be made to feel that he was being shown undue respect. A general could seldom be made to feel that he was being shown anything. On Governors Island, New York, where I was stationed for a year, it was my good fortune never to serve as officer of the day, in charge of emergencies. A friend of mine named Swardlow drew that duty on the day of the big blackout of 1965, when electrical power went out all over New York City and its environs. Governors Island lies just below the downtown tip of Manhattan. Swardlow looked out his window, saw the Wall Street skyline go dark, and immediately heard the phone ring. "Brief me," said the voice of a general.

Swardlow was at a loss. "We still have phone communications, sir," was all he could think to say. The general was outraged.

In saluting a general the trick was to wait, perhaps humming tunelessly as he bore down, until the last split second before he could legitimately bring you up on charges of ignoring him. Since a general didn't want to admit the possibility that it would enter into anyone's mind to ignore him, you had a certain amount of slack to work with. It was bracing to feel that you had frustrated a general for even a moment.

You could also say to a general, "Good morning, sir," quite confidently, at, say, 1900 hours. I found that a general so addressed would never exclaim, "Good God, Lieutenant, it's getting dark!" If some general had, I could have looked at him blankly and said, "Yes, sir," and I doubt he could have made a case stand up against me in any proper court-martial.

That's the way I handled generals at Governors Island, where in those days (the coast guard has it now) First Army Headquarters was based. Because so many generals came and went there, and because I never had to brief any of them, their effect was like that of Norse gods on someone raised a Methodist: entertaining. For the second half of my tour, however, I was transferred to Fort Totten, New York, in Queens, where there was only one general. He was often alluded to as The General. He gave the impression from a distance of being that uncommon sort of officer who could have made it as a sergeant if he'd wanted to. I developed a fear that he would enter into my life.

It was at Fort Totten that Emmy, a white cat, came through our kitchen window one day fully grown: a sizable, fleecy, impure but robust Persian, fluffy even to the bottoms of her feet. No one could say where she had come from. She took up with us, and soon became widely known on the post for all the things she was seen chasing. "If it moves, run it up the flagpole" was her attitude.

There was a pheasant whose periodic appearances from out of the woods bordering Fort Totten made him something of a post institution; Emmy chased him through a softball game. The paper girl, collecting at our door one evening, looked over at Emmy admiringly and said, "She chases all the *doougs*." A captain's wife reported having seen Emmy scooping something up out of Little Neck Bay "and struggling with it."

Emmy would also chase, or at least run out at, officers emerging from the Regional Air Defense Command building at close of day. She would lie in wait under the Command building until they came down the front steps. Like a big, somehow sinewy powder puff she would pounce and light right in front of them and then scurry back to her hiding place, having shaken their composure. But The General did not rattle easily. He took a shine to her.

I didn't work in the Command building, but we were quartered right across from it. Through our kitchen window I would see The General poking playfully at Emmy with his swagger stick and hear him calling her "WP," which stands for white phosphorus, a particularly loathsome kind of explosive. She would loll when he came at her, and then she would slap at his stick. Once, she and I were out walking. Emmy was the only cat I ever had who would go on long walks with me, and keep up; but she always acted as if she only happened to be heading in the same direction I was. We passed the garden-plot area. There was The General, digging. I veered toward a grove of trees, but Emmy ran over to him. As I looked on, frozen, she wet his mustard greens. It didn't faze him. Word did get around that he disapproved of her chasing the pheasant, whose appearance in some way pleased him, but months passed and he never took that matter, or any other, up with me.

Then one afternoon I was outside in full uniform hanging diapers. Regulations prohibited doing such a thing without changing into fatigues or civilian clothes, but I was in a hurry because the diapers had to be dry before the hour at which, pursuant to post regulations, you couldn't have any laundry in view.

So I was contending with a flapping damp diaper and a high-tension clothespin when I caught a glimpse out of the corner of my eye of a specialist 6 approaching with a gleam in his.

When a superior fails to notice that you are saluting him, you are supposed to say "By your leave, sir," and he is supposed to look up and return your salute. I had the clothespin and the diaper in my hands, and my hat was resting unevenly on my head, and I was pivoting slowly so as to keep my back always to the advancing spec 6, when I heard him say, "By your lea— YO!"

Emmy had made her only recorded spring at an enlisted man, and had timed it perfectly. I said, "Carry on, soldier," with relish, over my shoulder, and made to get on with my work.

Then I saw The General coming up the hill from the other direction. It was the closest I had seen him. He was one of those people who are overweight but stay in pretty good shape by dint of the vigor it takes to carry themselves as if in excellent shape. He appeared to be bursting out of his uniform. Wind caught the diaper and wrapped it around my head.

Well, maybe I should have peeled that diaper off forthrightly, faced up to The General, and cried:

"Sir! I shouldn't be here. I got married too young and I don't believe in the war. I want to be skinny-dipping and taking consciousness-exfoliating mushrooms with someone who looks like Grace Slick."

I just stood there. Obliquity saved me. Just as I did not want to admit to myself that I was in the army, The General may not have wanted to admit to himself that I was either. Or maybe Emmy struck a pose so beguiling to The General's eye that he was loath to spoil the moment by taking into account a diapered lieutenant. (She may have represented to him a freedom beyond even a general's: she could be soft, she could be fierce, she could simply choose.) Either way, he must have angled his eyes so as to make it credible, even to himself, that I was not in his field of vision.

"Quite some cat!" I heard The General say to the spec 6. "Got a bit of the devil in her."

"Yes, sir!" I heard the spec 6 say.

When I unwrapped my head, they were all three gone.

The next time I saw Emmy, I told her, with, I am afraid, some reediness of tone, "Quite some cat is right." She was intent on something under an armored personnel carrier and didn't return my salute.

What if I had buttonholed The General, and a dialectic had been wrought: I accepting that America was not cut out for a state of nature, he that napalming Asian peasants was not going to liberate them. The spec 6 might have joined in and reminded us that at heart this was a nation of shifting and mingling middle, not rapidly diverging upper and lower, classes. Together we might have charted a wholesome course toward the seventies, and the eighties might have had some soul.

But how often do people really face up to each other, flush? And how well does it turn out when they do? We are all slanty-eyed.

Even John Wayne in *The Sands of Iwo Jima.* On liberty, and planning to get polluted and fight some MPs because he is divorced and his son never writes him, he meets a quite attractive and decent-seeming woman named Mary in a bar. She gets him to lighten up a bit, and takes him to her apartment.

The two of them see something in each other — in the sixties it would have been no cheap encounter. But at her place, from a back room, a cry is heard. It's a baby. Nice-looking kid, well taken care of. Mary is picking up soldiers, inferably talking to them nude, and getting money from them so she can feed the baby — whose father, she tells Wayne when he asks, is "gone." She adds, "There are a lot tougher ways of making a living than going to war."

Oof. Wayne gets that grim-wry look in the corners of his eyes, softens and toughens all at once, tosses all his cash to the baby in the crib, and moves his essentially compassionate gruffness to the doorway, which he fills.

"You're a very good man," Mary tells him.

Looking off, Wayne vouchsafes a quick, grave near-grin. "You can get odds on that in the Marine Corps," he rumbles, and then he moves on toward Iwo Jima.

Women have told me that I am too oblique. "Tell it to John Wayne," I should have replied. All these years, and it has only just lately begun to occur to me: if he is so good, how come he can't keep any loved ones? Here he is, putting distance between himself and the very things — women and children — whose absence is driving him to drink.

What if Mary's cat had done a quick figure-eight around John Wayne's ankles, causing him to stand there in the doorway for a while and then to come back and sit on the couch; and the cat had jumped up next to him and stared at the side of his head intently, the way cats will do, and caused him to reflect.

We may think of cats as oblique, because by our standards there is an odd cast in their eyes. But insofar as a cat is interested at all, a cat is at least as un-hung-up and up-front as the sixties. If a cat spoke, a cat would say things like, "Hey. I don't see the *problem* here."

64

What if this cat had moved John Wayne to reflect, "Yuh know . . . the truth of the matter is, gettin' shot by people, and burnin' 'em alive . . . It's a tougher dollar than bringin' 'em home with you for . . . intimacies and . . . considerations. And — dag burn it, it's less *savory*. Now, I'm not sayin' what you do is *right*, but . . ."

And Mary had seen his point, and then . . . I believe *The Sands of Iwo Jima* would have had a healthier formative effect on me if John Wayne had petted the cat, and exchanged looks with it, and done the same with Mary, and she had undressed. I *like* it when women undress in movies — okay, it has been run into the ground, but I'm glad it got started.

And John Wayne had said, "I've got something else to get off my chest. You know how, a lot of times, I am aware of something that other people aren't, something that can't be told, so that I have to appear less caring than I am? And a lot of times . . . like in *The Man Who Shot Liberty Valance,* I let it be believed that Jimmy Stewart shot Liberty Valance, when actually *I* did, but that's all right; but I *also* let Jimmy have the woman I love, because . . . well, because even though he can't handle a gun, he's better for her than I am."

"Oh, who says?"

"Well, the thing of it is . . . Here's the thing: I can't get over the notion that honchos and women aren't *right* for each other."

"That's not *true.*"

"Oh, no? Why do you think I gravitate toward raw recruits? You can *get on* a raw recruit, that's why. The way you can't with a nude woman. You can *bark* at a raw recruit — in such a way that it's tougher'n hell but six months later the raw recruit, well, he realizes it was for his own good. To a raw recruit you can say — excuse me — you can say, 'You better shape your ass up, mister!' That doesn't work with a nude woman."

"Well . . ."

"Yeah, and nude women always want you to say such obvious things! Things that kinda go without saying: 'You have beautiful breasts and I love to touch them!' Well, I'm touching them, aren't I?"

"Mm . . ."

"Nude women think it's easy to talk to a nude woman. It's not! It's so personal! And there's a woman present!"

"Yes, but . . ."

"It's *hard.*"

"I know. Shhh. I know."

And after a while Mary had added, "Isn't this better than bashing and being bashed by MPs?"

"Well . . . *yeah. Sure* it is."

And still later Mary had made the observation that people should not enter upon a family ("or a war," John Wayne had put in) until they have talked nude with enough members of the opposite sex ("or nationality") to dispel some of that virulent *defensiveness* that cats don't have.

I know what would have happened the next morning, though. Because it happened to me in civilian life, with a brand-new leather jacket, not long after I got divorced. John Wayne and Mary would have waked, stretched, smiled a little abashedly at each other, reached for their clothes, and found that Mary's cat had sprayed foully — and that stuff will not come out — on John Wayne's Marine Corps tunic.

Frankly, having been in the situation myself and having given some thought to what he would do in it, I don't think John Wayne could have come up with an expression in the corners of his eyes potent enough to return that salute. I think he would have tried to murder the cat, and Mary would have screamed and the baby would have waked up and screamed and John Wayne would have screamed and the cat would have screamed, lap dissolve to beachhead, projectiles shrieking.

What *is* the problem?

Getting to the Bottom of Women's Underwear

ISN'T everyone into women's underwear? In some sense. Reaching out toward it, wearing it, designing it, something. Women have now even managed to make men's underwear interesting. By adopting it. After a fashion. Yes, women are wearing little brief Jockey-type shorts, and boxer-type shorts (which they call "tap pants," a term that may have something to do with the verb "to hit on") and undershirts instead of bras.

In some versions, the boxers have fly fronts. It is all right with me if women want to wear fly fronts. (What I wish is that more things for men had fly fronts — I am thinking of sweatpants and jockstraps. A jockstrap could have a Velcro fly, couldn't it? Have you ever tried to take a leak in — that is, while wearing — sweatpants and a jockstrap? It is enough to make you shrink from the fitness craze.)

I think the main reason designers build fly fronts into women's drawers is to make things awkward for the male underwear critic. There is an adversary relationship between underwear designers and underwear critics, and no one will ever win a Pulitzer in underwear criticism if he backs off from the hard questions, such as what to say about women's drawers that have fly fronts. Nor will anyone win a

Pulitzer if he says the obvious — that women's drawers with fly fronts certainly do not have a certain famous drawback that panty hose have.

Women, if they dust, use men's underwear to dust with. Whereas women's underwear makes men's heads swim. As long as that situation holds, and I do not see a radical shift on the horizon, we are a long way from unisexualism.

Women's underwear has names like panties, scanties, undies, bloomers, bikinis, frillies, teddies, camisoles, flimsies, G-strings (according to *Vogue,* G-strings are selling like hotcakes), and intimate apparel. Women's underwear comes in colors such as shell pink, lapis, ivory, jonquil, blush, and nude. Nude. That is a *color* that you see in women's underwear ads. For all I know there are now nude Crayolas.

It seems to me that the most erotic phrase in women's clothing is "nothing on underneath." When you come to underwear, that goes without saying. William Faulkner was inspired to write *The Sound and the Fury* by the sight of a girl hanging in a pear tree, her underpants showing. It seems to me that *The Sound and the Fury* was the least he could do.

What is the poem you remember most vividly from childhood? For me, two of them are locked in a dead heat: "I see London, I see France, / I see somebody's underpants. . . . There's a place in France, / Where the women wear no pants."

It gets my goat when women blame the arms race on men. Men are only struggling to come up with something half as potent as a pair of simple nonabbreviated pink panties whose extremely pullable-looking thin waistband stretches just below the navel. Nobody has ever really improved upon that basic panty.

Nobody has improved upon the '54 Chevrolet either, but new cars and new underwear have to be sold before the old ones wear out. Or this country will go right down the tubes.

So men have to go into stores, look saleswomen in the eye, and ask for women's underwear. This is always good for a laugh. To obviate the embarrassment factor, according to a recent news account, "a number of boutiques have instituted men-only nights, sometimes held at local bars." Count me out of those, thanks. "Hey, Murph, you gonna buy one of them tea-colored floral nylon lace teddies so sheer it practically floats on the body?" "Hail no, Vinnie, it's me for a set of them powder-blue wispies with the labial rosettes." "Har, har, har." "Whoooo!" Then people start fighting.

Do you know that there is a line of women's underwear called Titcha? That's right. I saw an ad for it in *Vogue*. The model was wearing a black bra whose cup area was see-through except for a sprinkling of black flower petals and a black spot in the middle with a see-through spot in the middle of the black spot. I am not describing it very evocatively, but you see the point.

You know how Titcha is supposedly pronounced? According to the ad? "Say it softly — 'Tee-sha.' " Right! Right! Sure! Whom do these people think they are pulling the leg of?

Not the leg of the underwear critic. The underwear critic sees through that kind of thing. The underwear critic knows that all underwear advertising is intended quite simply to make men start saying "Hammadahammadahammada."

The underwear critic refuses to be lured into sexism. The underwear critic does not focus upon these "you-shaped" and "next-to-nothing" and "girly-girl-look" bits of fabric. Nor does he focus upon the bodies of the models who are lounging about in one or another "light, soft underlayer." He focuses upon what these women must be like, as persons.

You take a model who is wearing a trim silky-lacy double-clasp bra and Lollipop panties. Lollipop panties! That's what they call them! And pearls. A model like that is probably a person who says, "Oh, my goodness!" She has nice china, from her grandmother. I would probably chip it.

Okay. So you take a model who wears black slinky stuff and a garter belt with black stockings. I am going to confess something to you. I never knew anybody who, to the best of my knowledge, dressed like that. Underwear critics do not hang out with people like that. Or it may be that people who might dress like that in the company of other people do not dress like that when they are with underwear critics.

Now take a model who wears bikini Jockey shorts and one of those cutaway undershirts, the kind Italian men used to wear while sitting around the table. A model like that is probably what is called today "an active person," which is a euphemism for someone who will wear your ass out. On the other hand, it would probably not cost an arm and a leg to buy this person some underwear for Valentine's Day, if she did not insist on designer labels. You are always looking up to see a person like this running past the window. But she has to stop running sometime. And when she does, she is what they call "at ease with her body." Sort of a military term. Such a person deserves a salute. Pre-sent . . . arms.

You see the kind of trap an underwear critic can fall into.

Once, years ago, I met an extraordinarily fine-looking person at a party. "What do you do?" I asked.

"I model lingerie," she said.

"Lord have mercy!" is what I wanted to say, but I knew that would be gauche. I made an effort, first to stop my mouth from hanging open, and then to regard her in a cool manner. She misinterpreted.

"So, automatically, I don't have anything to say, right?" she said.

"Whanh?" I replied.

"I'm a model, so therefore I must not have anything to say."

I didn't have anything to say. What I said was, "Oh, no, I'm sure you . . . have, ah, lots of things to say."

"Like what?" she said.

I didn't know.

What I had failed to do was put myself in her place. I had regarded her as a person about whom it was appropriate to reflect, *Can you imagine what she looks like in lingerie?*

What men ought to realize in this day and age is, hell, I don't know. But let us say that what men ought to realize in this day and age is that women wear underwear not to look a certain way but to *feel* a certain way.

What a man ought to do with that realization is another question. A question not for underwear critics but for active persons who don't let things slow down long enough for questions to arise.

It is a wise underwear critic who accepts that there are fundamental mysteries that he cannot break down, that lie underneath the "underneath" in "nothing on underneath."

I am looking at an ad for Maidenform "Sweet Nothings." "Sweet Nothings" include "camisole and pettis" and "front-close bras" (see, if I'd written that ad I might have called them "front-open bras"). The ad copy reads: "Sweet Nothings are feminine, exquisite, delicate, enchanting, lacy, and lovely. In short, Sweet Nothings are quite something. Just like the dreams they inspire."

In this ad, a model wearing various hints of blue is lolling calmly amid frilly bedding, hand mirrors, perfume bottles, and flowers. In one picture she's wearing a gossamer film of a dress, she is sitting on a rock beside a sylvan body of water, and she is gazing composedly into the rapt eyes of a man who looks like a younger Gary Hart who doesn't need her vote. Her hair is perfect throughout.

I think what this ad has in mind is women's dreams. As opposed to men's. I don't recall ever having a dream that had any very highly defined underwear in it. What *are* pettis, anyway?

Let us get it straight that women wear certain kinds of underwear for the sake of their own dreams. Let us also bear this in mind: you may start your day with a cup of black coffee, a glass of gin, and a jigger of hot sauce, but until you have been looped into a woman's dreams, you don't know anything.

Erma Gets Down

WHOSE role do housework and child care fit into best, in this time of sexual reapportionment? All I know is that they have often fit into my role like live roosters into a sack, and I love Erma Bombeck. I'll tell you why.

When I was a youth my mother, who at least by today's standards waited on me hand and foot, and whose sense of humor and of everything else was intense, tried to interest me in various housewifely humorists who gave her solace. They always made me want to say what I remember Richard Pryor, in the role of Lightning Bug Johnson, telling Lily Tomlin, in the role of the Tasteful Lady, when the two of them were trapped in an elevator. The T.L. tried to relieve the tension with a bit of tasteful whimsy. L.B. cringed. "If I told people I know a joke like that," he said, "they'd beat me to death."

Bombeck, however, can get down. She has produced eight books with titles like *The Grass is Always Greener over the Septic Tank,* whose staggering sales I do not resent. There are best-selling humorists who do get my goat. Andy Rooney springs to mind. Wry. Who needs wry? I haven't got *time* for wry. I'm too busy trying to fix the toilet, which I discovered didn't work when I emptied the Kitty Litter into it, which I had to do because it was causing the entire first floor of the house to smell like the cat had died in it — I wish — nine times. Everyone else in the house had solved the problem by going upstairs. I don't know what the cat can have eaten. Usually I know exactly what the cat has eaten. Not only have I fed it to the cat, at the cat's keen insistence, but the cat has thrown it up on the rug and someone has tracked it all the way over onto the other rug. I don't know why cats are such habitual vomiters. They don't seem to enjoy it, judging by the sounds they make while doing it. Every so often cats say to themselves, "Well, time to vomit," and then they do. It's in their nature. A dog is going to bark, a cat is going to vomit.

If I offend you, I'm sorry. But these problems exist. It is no good sweeping cat vomit under the rug. As all of us who work at home know and Erma Bombeck conveys so well, no matter how modern women or men get — well, it will never be modern enough. But what I was going to say is, someone will always have to keep the home, and the home is not pretty.

For one thing, there are far too frequently children in it. Bombeck gets them right:

"SON: She's doing it again.

"FATHER: Doing what?

"SON: Humming.

"DAUGHTER: I am not humming.

"SON: You are so. There, she did it again, Dad. Watch her neck. She's humming so no one can hear her but me."

Children do unconscionable things, and Erma Bombeck knows it. Once when she was sleeping, "they put a hamster on my chest and when I bolted upright (my throat muscles paralyzed with fright) they asked, 'Do you have any alcohol for the chemistry set?' "

Not that mothers are any bargain. Bombeck:

" 'You talk about dental work,' said a small blonde. 'Come here, George. Open your mouth, George.' The lights

73

danced on George's metal-filled mouth like Ali Baba's cave. 'That,' she said emphatically, 'is my mink stole. A mother's sacrifice. And is he grateful? He is not.' "

I am not going to tell you that Bombeck is among our most polished stylists. Lapses on the order of those lights dancing like a cave do crop up. As do sentences like this one, which explains how she figured a box of cereal cost her $116.53: "This included repairing my tooth, which I chipped on a nuclear submarine in the bottom of the box, throwing part of the cereal to the birds in the snow, necessitating antibiotics, and the cost of packing, shipping, and crating it through three moves." She is not what I would call unrelievedly hilarious, and I was not blown away by some of her serious declarations of what she wants from her children: "I want you to be a cornball, a real honest-to-God, flag-waving cornball, who, if you must march, will tell people what you are for, not what you are against."

But her humor has a nice no-nonsense tone. She knows that in fact life is not cornball. (What is a cornball, anyway? Maybe that's what that last thing the cat threw up on the rug was.) And she is a fine exaggerator:

" 'Isn't there another way you could get to the card club?' he asked.

" 'Yes,' I replied. 'I could tape peanuts to my arms and maybe attract enough pigeons to fly me there, but I'd rather drive the car.' "

Bombeck "used to shuffle through the house saying, 'Who am I? Where am I going?' All I did was scare the Avon lady half to death." Trying to be a modern, on-the-go woman, she finds herself rushing about, "trying to quick-thaw a chop under each armpit. . . ."

She wonders why a child will "eat yellow snow" but won't drink from his brother's glass.

When she mentions a film her kids see at school, it is exactly right: *The History of Sulfur.*

She knows someone who is so caught up in stamps that

she has "glue-breath." "In desperation, we even switched to a newly formed church across town that gave 120 trading stamps each time we attended. (We now worship a brown and white chicken with a sunburst on its chest.)"

I think Bombeck would appeal to readers of all genders even had there been no women's movement. But now that men's roles have gone all to hell, and every modern person who is not rich or vagrant is half housewife, we can perhaps take Bombeck's undespairing desperation more to heart. In my household, for instance, *I* seem to be the only person who understands how to replace a toilet-paper spindle. Bombeck in regard to this matter is on the money.

For my part, here is something I don't understand. Children take their shoes off whenever they step inside the house. Why is this? It doesn't slow down the outgrowing process. When you take off your shoes your feet get cold, if you're normal, and you catch your little toe on hard metal things. Whenever I want a child to go out into the snow and get the groceries out of the car, the child is standing there barefooted as a yard dog, as my mother would have said (I wish she were alive to discuss this with, except that she would probably say, "Just be thankful your children have feet"), and I know that by the time the child gets resocked and shod the groceries will have mildewed.

This is a problem that bothers me more than the mounting federal deficit. And much as I esteem Doris Lessing, it is not she whose thinking I would like to hear on this.

Back to BBs

WHY do people want to technologize children? Some years ago I read about a kids' BB-gun tournament in Clarkesville, Tennessee. The contestants went through their BBs one by one. Occasionally they would throw one away. "The idea is to find ten exactly the same," said a spokesman for the Daisy Air Rifle company. "These are our best BBs. Regular BBs vary from .173 to .175 caliber. Precision shot used in competition is .175. Still, you'll find some bad ones."

Three hundred crack-shot boys and girls aged seven to fourteen, amid shushed adult spectators and under the hovering supervision of Jaycees and Daisy people, spent the weekend of the Fourth of July at the International BB Gun Championship matches, firing thousands of just-right BBs from guns costing thirty dollars apiece. The guns, modified by coaches, were all but silent. The BBs floated softly, sometimes failing to go through the thin silver-dollar-sized cardboard targets. A quiet, flawless, slow-moving BB is a highly accurate BB.

The afternoons that weekend in Tennessee were devoted to what the sponsors called recreation. I thought BB-shooting itself was supposed to be recreation. "We want this to be a total experience," said the Daisy man. "We care about the human being." Maybe some group ought to run an International Total Experience Championship.

A lot of parents I know refuse to let their kids have any kind of toy guns. I think that's repressive. The first time my son saw his older cousin Stuart's BB gun, his eyes took on a glow. My daughter, who will try her hand at anything, could take Stuart's BB gun or leave it alone, but she could shoot it straight. It turns out that in competition girls tend to be better BB shots than boys. They are said to relax easier. Maybe they don't dwell upon the overtones involved.

If I had spent as much of my childhood studying French as I did shooting a BB gun, I would have been prepared to go directly from grammar school to Paris and open a shop. I wasn't picky about my BBs; in fact I would dig them out of trees and shoot them again. I had a Red Ryder carbine, unmodified except for various dents and rust spots and the cocking mechanism's tendency to jam. This malfunction probably developed from my fondness for pulling the trigger with the cocking lever open, causing the lever to whang shut violently. I don't know why that gave me such satisfaction, but it did. When fired properly my gun went *punh* and sometimes shot true enough to puncture the chicken-pie tin or knock over the cylindrical cardboard BB container I was aiming at. I pretended I was a pioneer shooting at Indians. My politics, I realize now, were crude.

I even engaged in a couple of group BB-gun battles. These mostly entailed creeping around in the woods, but it was considered fair, if you were careful, to shoot another participant in the behind. This stung, and seemed wrong as we did it, and worked off forever my desire to shoot somebody like in the movies. My friend Francis Rowe once shot his BB gun at a blue jay and it actually fell from the tree and landed at our feet. We felt abruptly grave, and I think even briefly discussed religion. I had shot at squirrels and blue jays to scare them out of our fig tree, but had never actually *hit* one. The blue jay wasn't dead yet. My friend tried to get me to end its misery — it was staring in our direction — but I couldn't. Finally he did. I haven't shot at a bird since, except some ducks near Waco, Texas, with a shotgun. To clean the freshly shot ducks, we cut them open from the tail end, gave them a fling while holding on to their necks, and then reached up into the body cavity to pull out the guts. It felt red-hot in there. I haven't shot at anything living since then. Once I went goose-hunting, and had a good time, and fired when everyone else did, and got a kick out of firing, but I didn't aim at anything — certainly not geese.

And if I ever saw my kids shooting other kids in the pants I would, of course, be horrified and move to stop them, as my parents would have done if they had seen me. So it is not in the interest of wild gunplay that I decry the International BB Gun Championship. I decry it because it seems like the kind of thing a kid would want to escape from, not into. A great many of the things that seemed to me most worth doing as a child were things of which an adult, had one been watching me do them, would have said, "What do you want to do *that* for?" and I wouldn't have answered.

Throwing mud clods is actually more fun, and better exercise, than shooting BBs. Why not an International Mud Clod Throwing Championship? One reason is that nobody sells mud clods, but I don't begrudge the Daisy people — who made my Red Ryder and whose name is nice — their promotional interest in this event.

I just don't see what value there is in it for the shooters. I don't see why a kid would want to go hang around with a bunch of Jaycees under carefully controlled conditions, for the sake of precisely quantified and certified target scores, when he could be out somewhere by himself or with friends shooting at a bird, actually hitting it, looking the bird in the eye with a wild surmise, regretting it all, and learning something. And not knowing what, exactly.

One Man's Response to a Question Posed by *Mademoiselle*

"As Men, What Do We Think We Need from Women, How Does What We Say We Need Coincide with or Differ from What We *Really* Need?"

I HAVE looked deeply into my heart on this one, and then looked quickly away. I hate looking deeply into my heart. It's like looking deeply into my filing system. Or my garage. There are interesting things in my garage — just for starters, three chickens walking around loose — but you wouldn't ever want to go in there and try to sort them all out.

But here is what I am inclined to believe. Just speaking for myself. I am inclined to believe that I don't need the same things from all women. What I need from the woman I hand my dirty shirts to is not what I need from an ideal wife, say. What I need from the woman I hand my dirty shirts to is no starch and on hangers. I hate starch. But employees of laundering concerns tend to say to themselves, "Well, he probably doesn't mean 'no starch' like, you know, *no* starch. He probably means 'not a whole lot of starch.' But I think he'll look perkier with, oh, about a pound and a half of starch."

On hangers I can usually get, but no starch is like pulling teeth. Incidentally, I had a woman dentist when I was a boy.

How many of your so-called new males can make that claim? I liked the way her fingers tasted.

What I need from an ideal wife — well, I should mention that I have been pretty busy myself lately trying to remember what it was that I was trying to think of a couple of weeks ago, because I have the feeling I am about ready to think of it now if I could only remember what it was. Also, I have been tied up with all the consideration I've been devoting to the idea of doing something about my filing system.

What I need from an ideal wife is for her to go into my mind . . .

No, that is asking too much. Say you are an ideal husband. Can you imagine what it would be like to go into your actual wife's mind? You'd be saying, "What is this pile of stuff over here?"

And she would be saying, "Oh, well, that's just — never mind, I'll go through that later."

"You *say* you will, but . . . Okay, what is this cruddy old dingbat here? Let's throw it out."

"Cruddy! No! I want to keep that."

"Why? What possible use could you have for it?"

"Well, I'm fond of it. It's . . . you know."

"I *don't* know. What *is* it?"

"Well, it's . . . my idea of you."

"What!?"

What I need from an ideal wife is for her to go into my filing system . . . No, that is asking too much.

What I need from an ideal wife is for her to go into the garage (there!) and sort everything out. (She was the one who wanted chickens.) Let me put it this way: I am not holding my breath. Except when I get too close to the garage.

Which brings up something that men may reasonably expect from women: that they smell better than men. By that, I mean that they have a higher sense of smell. In a recent study at the University of Pennsylvania, women on the average outperformed men in odor identification tests at all ages. So why am I always the one who is finally driven to empty the Kitty Litter?

Of course if one's wife's olfaction were more ideal, then one's own effluvium might have to be. I don't know that any Ivy League school has done a study on this, but I think it is generally accepted that men tend to reek more than women do, on the average. Isn't that just like nature? Making one sex smell worse and the other more acutely?

What does nature *want*, anyway?

Mind you, I'm not saying it's women's fault. In fact I'm . . .

Wait a minute.

Wait a minute; wait a minute.

Am I being sandbagged here? I thought it was sexist to suggest that men need anything in particular from women that they don't need from men. I thought what a liberated woman was supposed to say when a man asked her to go up-stairs and come down wearing nothing but a pair of fluffy pink house shoes was, "Because I'm a woman, right? Get your friend Ed to do it." I thought a person was a person now.

On second thought, however, I guess things have lately come around to the point where men don't always have to be skittish about saying something that discriminates. If you ask me, a lot of the credit for that should go to President and Mrs. Reagan. I know I find it very hard to think of either one of them in terms of, you know, a person, as such.

So, what the heck. If I'm out of line here, tell me. (That last sentence is a good example of something men say to women that doesn't coincide closely with what men think they really need.) But here's what I think:

What men really need is for women to have more sense than men do.

Let me give you an illustration. A man is sitting home staring off into space, of an evening, and all of a sudden he springs up, slaps his head, and exclaims to his significant other (who is, I don't know, knitting, whittling, restructuring a holding company):

"Hey! I've got it! Wouldn't it be a neat idea if I invented this magnetic chemical so strong that a tiny drop of it in Cincinnati would attract a freight train all the way from Dayton? And then I could develop a piping system whereby we could pipe this chemical beneath all the streets of Moscow — see, the great thing is, the Russians have all their radar pointing *up* — so we could sit down at the negotiating table and kind of lean back in our chairs for a minute or two, smiling and listening to all their rantings, and then we could shift forward suddenly, with narrowed eyes, and snap: 'Can it. Here's the deal. You come to your senses and drop all this Communist malarkey right now, and give us Cuba back. Or else.'

"And the Russians sputter for a minute and then they get very still and say, 'Or else what?'

"And we smile again. And lean back in our chairs again. And say, in this casual tone, 'Ohhh, or else we will open the little pores in the pipes that at this moment are in place beneath all the streets of your capital city, thereby releasing this magnetic chemical that is so strong it will pull you, by the nails in your shoes, *down into the earth* up to about midcalf level the minute you set foot out of the Kremlin. *Then* try to keep some kind of crazy godless economy afloat.'

"Wouldn't that be neat?"

Okay.

What this man *thinks* he needs from this woman is for her to answer, "Yes, dear, I suppose so."

No, I take that back. What he *thinks* he needs from her is for her eyes to sparkle as she answers, breathily, "Oooo, *yes!*"

What he *says* he needs from her is for her to give him some thoughtful, objective feedback on this thing.

What he *really* needs is for her to say, "No."

Why?

Not because a man (or a woman) needs the consolation of saying to himself/herself, "There is no telling how far I could go if it weren't for Ms. [Mr.] Cold Light of Dawn over here."

But rather because a man needs for a woman to help him understand the limitations of "Get them by the balls and their hearts and minds will follow."

There may also be something along those lines that a woman needs from a man. But I haven't sorted it out yet.

New Renaissance Lyrics

I
From Celia

Come, my Arthur, finish up
With that saucer and that cup.
Now that I'm a realtor,
I'm not moody anymore.

Elbow-deep in suds you stand,
Art, my sweet dish-doing man.
Now that we have traded roles,
Let us haste to merge our souls.

You're in housework, I'm in houses.
Ev'ry move you make arouses
Me to seize the fruits of love.
Come, peel off your rubber glove,

Then — no, no, forget the laundry.
Turn the lights down, play an André
Kostelanetz tape, and we'll
Close our new domestic deal.

II
To Jane's Mind

When from aerobic exercise you rise,
You are no fairer, Jane, nor am I fonder.

For what I love in you is not your thighs
But how your forehead wrinkles when you ponder.

Other women may have higher pectoral
Development and glutei more taut.
They lack your expertise on the electoral
College and the state of modern thought.

And when you raise a complex current issue,
You're always penetrating, always apt.
The times I want most eagerly to kiss you
Are when in chess I find you've got me trapped.

The books that I can't fathom, Jane, you memorize.
I never *get* the jokes *you* think are cheap.
You scoff at films that dazzle my poor dimmer eyes,
And now you've learned Italian in your sleep.

So though I'm glad you limber up your frame, dear,
The thing that makes me hurtle through the ozone
Like Santa Claus behind his merry reindeer
Is just to see your mind without its clothes on.

III
To a Shy Person She Has Had Her Eye On

Bob, if I were twenty-four
Maybe I'd be charmed by your
Tendency to hint around.
But I doubt it. I have found,
In fullness of maturity,
That whatsoever's said to me
Might just as well be said outright,
Right now — a modern woman's quite
Prepared to hear what modern men
May have in mind. So try me; then

I'll let you know if I can see
How we can cheat mortality.
I hate mortality, don't you?
You do? You'll *say* you do? You'll do.

Let Me Count the Ways (39)

Hey, to me, all women are sexy. Right? All breathing women. If they want to be. As far as I'm concerned. I mean where do I get off, picking and choosing, setting standards? What gives me the right?

Just because everyone is abuzz about my head-turning cameo in the ground-breaking new movie *Plough,* with what's-her-name who looks so much like Jessica Lange? Just because I am built like a damn moose? Just because my wavy pepper-and-salt hair cascades down my back to where, if it went one quarter-inch further, you'd have to say I was a poof (but it doesn't)? Just because the person whom I retain to keep that cascade precisely *au point* with tiny tungsten scissors is (her own idea) a lapsed, monokinied Shiite woman who weeps with shame? Just because it has come out recently that I share a small but elegantly appointed motor home with (the Iranian aside) three not only mouth-watering but also constantly (in a sophisticated way) salivating honeybunches (if the term offends, I withdraw it), one of whom has been known to sport pince-nez but no pants and the other two of whom are teenaged Polynesian twins, Awanna and M'tou, who raise and fight bulldogs on the side?

Just for these and many other reasons, you expect me to

put myself in the awkward position of sitting down and taking pen in hand and laying my heart bare in order to tell you "What Makes a Woman Sexy"?

Well, all right. But not for those reasons.

I am going to do it — and I am going to do it with candor, and I am going to do it unflinchingly, and I am going to do it feelingly and straight — because I will do anything.

Well, anything I want to. Within reason. You never know these days what people think you mean, when you say "anything." I don't mean anything faithless, trashy, or painful.

So okay. Here are the 39 things that make a woman sexy:

1. If she has barbecue sauce on her mouth.

2. If she looks like she will do anything. That she wants to. That isn't faithless, trashy, or painful.

3. You'd be hard put to say exactly where one part of her body leaves off and the next begins. You can put your hand on her waist and it feels like all of her is going to pass through there eventually.

4. If her name is Rita. Think about it. Rita Hayworth, Rita Moreno, Rita Gam, Lovely Rita Meter Maid, Rita in the movie *Educating Rita.* And, what the heck (say you're a congressman or something), Rita Jenrette.

5. I'm going to skip over a few obvious ones here.

6. If she can make gravy.

7. If she appears to have a lot of sense. You know what I mean? Maybe what I mean is, if she knows what I mean. But no, it's more than that. You look at her and before you even get to know her you feel a certain gratitude, a certain peace. You feel that she is not going to spring some kind of unfairly inexplicable notion on you that you will never make any sense out of and that will wind up being your fault. You feel that she knows where the keys are. You feel that the two of you could give each other little looks to the effect that ah, yeah, *unh,* that's life.

8. If she appears not to have a lick of sense.

9. Some intriguing combination of a lot and not a lick.

10. If she is securely hooked up with a good friend of yours. With such a woman you can kid around and bump hips and even take a nip at each other's neck, in plain view or *not* in plain view, all the while feeling very good about knowing (a) that neither of you is going to do anything disloyal to your friend, and (b) that you will never have to get in an argument with this woman over why neither of you knows where the keys are. Then too, you never know, your friend might die.

11. By the same token, sort of: If she is a good friend of the woman you are securely hooked up with. Here again you can bump around guiltlessly, and in this case you are favoring the woman you are securely hooked up with by showing her friend that the woman you are securely hooked up with is not securely hooked up with some schlump.

12. Lips.

13. If she is not too thin and not too rich. "You can never be too thin or too rich" is the most self-serving remark of recent times except for "That camera doesn't lie" (Ronald Reagan). You can be so thin that you haven't got any sugar on you. (As a southern American white man, I am resigned to accepting blame for just about anything, but not by God anorexia.) And you can be so rich that nobody ever tells you that everybody thinks you are silly.

14. If her attitude toward her own physical presence is, "Hey, for whatever anybody else may think it's worth, I *got* it. And I can shake it. And if you're not interested who asked you?" Why in the world do women say things like, "Oh, I'm too droopy in the hiney and got hardly any chest and my legs are just *sticks*"? Unless they manage to say it provocatively. Sparkle goes a long way.

15. If she looks shapely in shapeless clothes.

16. If her hair looks like it looks naturally good without thousands of dollars' worth of treatments.

17. If she is naked as a jaybird. Okay, call me old-fashioned.

89

18. If she is a good sport but doesn't take any shit. (I realize this is a fine line.)

19. Fine lines. I mean, fine in simultaneously the sense of "exquisite" and "she's so fine." Not brittle lines. Flexible fine lines. (See 3, above.)

20. If she's barefooted. ("Barefoot" is cute, but "barefooted" is more down-to-earth.) It may be objected that this was covered by point 17, above, "naked as a jaybird," but it wasn't. "Barefooted" focuses on the whole matter of padding around. Ever listen to a woman's bare feet padding around upstairs? (Not slapping, not stomping, not dragging, but padding. Around.)

21. A sweetly robust way of laughing. And of sneezing.

22. I am going to skip over some more obvious ones here.

23. If she can have a good rowdy time engaging in dialectic. Doesn't want to be thesis continually nor indefatigably antithesis, but likes to mix it up with you and come out with something fresh.

24. There's a lot in how she pets a dog.

25. Good hands, generally.

26. When she's wet. Ideally with sweat, or with something else (gravy, for instance) involving an element of slickum. Swimming-pool or saltwater wetness is not fluid enough: the hand catches on it.

27. If she'd like to go run out into any available body of water right now, though.

28. If she looks like she is built for dancing but would just as soon kid around.

29. If there is nothing on God's green earth that would convince her to become a Republican. If she's already Republican, if she was raised that way, well, I don't have to know everything. I guess.

30. If she is slightly cross-eyed. Maybe I'm kinky. Maybe I don't like to be focused on too intensely. I don't know. But you know how Karen Black's eyes, and Lauren Hutton's, and to a lesser extent Ellen Barkin's, seem just out of true?

31. If she looks like she could go like Valerie Brisco-Hooks if she weren't so languorous.

32. If she's just naturally got coloring all over.

33. Or, on the other hand, if she's so pellucid beneath her clothes that it's like the beginning of time under there.

34. If she responds with informed warmth to at least ten of the following names: Dwight Gooden, Robert Montgomery, Patsy Cline, Earl Long, Christopher Smart, Willis Reed, Candy Barr, Les Paul, Judy Holliday, Dock Ellis, Cole Younger, Oliver St. John Gogarty, Mr. Kitzel, Grace Paley, Maynard G. Krebs, Nellie Fox, Myles Na Gopaleen, Mary Worth, Claudette Colbert, Grundoon, Zora Neale Hurston, Butch Thompson, Jeanette MacDonald, Keela the Outcast Indian Maiden, L. C. Greenwood, and Joel McCrea.

35. One of those T-shirts with the big, big armholes. You know what I mean? You keep hoping the flag will come along and she'll salute? Of course I realize that from a respect-for-women point of view those shirts are worn only for purposes of mobility and air-conditioning. Uh-huh.

36. If her slip is showing. Remember slips? Whatever happened to slips? It's such a great term: slip. Not too froufrou, not too stern.

37. Heart. My friend Jane Bell (see point 10, above), her husband, several other congenial people, and I were out lurching around happily one night in Nashville, having breakfast in a place with a greasy floor at 3:00 A.M. I mention the floor because Jane slipped on it and fell flat on her face. Jane has elegant, delicate features. One of her front teeth broke right half in two on a diagonal line. All of a sudden Jane was snaggletoothed. It was a revelation! She looked wonderful! Not that there were any flies on her before, by any means; she always looked *lovely*; but, I don't know, now she looked exotic, in a very down-home kind of way. A little bit evil, somehow; certainly a little bit trashy; all because of that slantwise gap in the middle of her mouth, which illumined the refinement of her features thereabout. We kept

telling her how great she looked. But the admirable thing was how well she took it. Many women — and Jane is admittedly not the most absolutely laid-back person in America, even when her teeth are even — would have cried, or fumed, or pouted, or blamed someone, or insisted on going home. Jane just went right along with the course of the evening. Accepted compliments, did not demand commiseration, looked *louche* on request, and even joined in the discussion of topics quite unrelated to her mouth. We were back at her house around six, and when I got up a few hours later I found, with some regret, that she had already been to a dentist (rustled up by her husband on a Sunday morning) who had restored her to simple elegance. And she was ready for brunch. Incidentally, I want to say something now that for some reason I have never told Jane to her face: pound for pound, she can hold more gin without getting bleary than anybody else I know.

38. If you've been together through a lot of ups and downs. And there was always a firm bounce on the bottom.

39. If she eats *all*, every bit, of the meat off her chicken bones.

Okay? Are you satisfied? Now I got to get these bulldogs off my leg. I get *no* rest.

The Phantom Jukebox

(A Recitation)

I entered that small Texas bar
For I had a mouthful of dust.
But I was so happy otherwise
I thought my heart would bust.

The public relations firm I owned
Had added two new clients.
And one sold plastic fishing worms,
The other a household appliance.

And I'd received a large bequest
From my old aunt, who'd died.
And though her passing touched us all,
I felt enhanced inside.

So I was in the mood to hear
Some easy-listening — a
Taste I shared with my new Swedish
Girl, whose name was Inge —

And other kinds of cheerful tunes,
And have some Scotch-and-waters.
So I approached the jukebox there
And jingled all my quarters.

I punched E-4, for "Loving You
Is Easy 'Cause You're Beautiful."
But what I heard was a country man's
Lament, sung through a snootful.

I tried to play a disco tune,
Then Tijuana Brass.
But what that jukebox played instead
Was "There Stands the Glass."

"Bartender!" I loudly cried,
"Your jukebox took my quarter,
But won't play what I want it to.
It must be out of order."

A look of sadness swept the face
Of that drink-serving man.
"Stranger," he said, "I think that you
Had better look again."

And when I turned my eyes back 'round,
Sad songs still filled the air.
My quarter, though, lay on the floor.
There was no jukebox there.

"Ten years ago tonight, you see,"
The genial barman sighed,
"The jukebox that we did have there
Played 'Faded Love' and died.

"The jukebox," he informed me then,
In a voice that came near choking,
"Loved our cigarette machine
That must have frowned on smoking.

"For it would not sell cigarettes.
We had to send it back.

As it was dollied out the door,
We heard that jukebox crack.

"And every year about this time,
The old jukebox appears.
The only songs that it will play
Fill all our hearts with tears.

"And late at night 'round closing time
Comes echoing the sound
Of falling packs of cigarettes
That never touch the ground."

The barman's face, I noticed then,
Was careworn and bizarre
And so were all the faces of
The patrons at the bar.

Three long years ago that was,
In fact this very night.
And since then things have changed for me,
Just as for you they might.

I've lost my p.r. comp'ny now,
And seen the last of Inge.
My money's gone, and old George Jones
Is now my favorite singer.

And all that I have left these days
Is country songs and woe —
Which I prefer to ecstasy
And Barry Manilow.

And when, at night, alone, I need
That old jukebox to hear,
All I have to do is drop
A quarter and a tear.

The Simple Life

Observe the protozoan swim.
It's not a her, it's not a him.
Its income, outgo both are slim.
It has no school or home or gym,
Or tears or blood or bile or phlegm.

A long way down from seraphim —
And yet it fills the interim
Between prelude and closing hymn
More gainfully than you do, Jim.
For when it dies it's two of them.

Real People, So to Speak

What's So Hot about Celebs?

"It is true," a great man once said,
"that I also have to pee, but for quite
different reasons."
— Tommaso Landolfi

A CELEBRITY is someone distinguished for having been heard of by a whole lot of people. Wherever a whole lot of people get together, there have to be plenty of conspicuous, plainly lettered signs posted to keep them all from wetting their pants and falling over one another. That's what a celebrity is: a sign saying I HAVE BEEN TELEVISED. YOU WANT MY AUTOGRAPH. The only difference is that a celebrity *causes* people to wet their pants and fall over one another. Even if he is Charles Nelson Reilly.

Fair enough, I guess. Only I remember a time when celebrities, like major-league baseball players, were fewer in number and you *knew* them. Maybe they weren't particularly accomplished, but they had done something more than garble their lines on purpose and grin more or less engagingly so as to appear on "Foul-ups, Bleeps, and Blunders." Maybe they were press agents' creations, but at least they felt obliged to display a measure of personality, however trumped up. They worked at fame — disrobed at openings, threw drinks on other celebrities, wore trademark toupees, stole wives.

99

But over the past decade or so, a celebrity has become someone whose name and/or face you have seen more than twice while flipping through magazines in the checkout-counter line or switching from channel to channel, searching in vain for intrinsic interest. You don't really care who they are, but — like certain French verbs when you are trying to satisfy your foreign-language requirement — they have popped up often enough that you feel vaguely as if you probably ought to know them.

Take the case of Julio Iglesias. I could not pick Julio Iglesias — by his face or by his voice — from a boatload of soccer players, and yet his name is lodged in my consciousness. Because he paid to have it lodged there.

Two years ago, Iglesias — a megastar Spanish crooner with a huge following in South America — regretted deeply that North America did not know him from a bale of hay. So he paid Rogers and Cowan, a p.r. megafirm, something like two million dollars to make him mega above the Rio Grande. America's Next Lover was what he wanted to be.

I don't love him. But I do know, and so do major numbers of other gringos, that he sang a duet with Willie Nelson on the Country Music Association awards show last year. (Andy Warhol's prophecy that eventually everyone will be famous for fifteen minutes may never pan out, but it does appear that everyone will in time sing a duet with Willie Nelson.) I don't know whether or not Rogers and Cowan arranged that performance, but I have heard the record that resulted when Willie and Julio went into the studio to do the song they sang on TV that night.

And when I heard it, I cried, "No, Willie! Sing a duet with Rosemary Clooney! Sing a duet with Freddy Fender! Sing a duet with any number of persons who, while working as many tough rooms as you have, became more good than celebrated! Do not sing a duet with this road-show Engelbert Humperdinck!"

But the thing had been done. Julio Iglesias was a giant in the industry.

It is no new development that fame is more lucrative than workmanship. But there used to be more of a connection between the two. It also used to be that when a President looked at the nation from the television screen, part of his expression said, "Well, hell, I'm doing the best I can. But being President is *hard*, goddamn it." Presidents strove to be real. Now we have a President whose forte is a knack for simplified celebrity.

In its tenth-anniversary issue, *People* magazine picked the top celebrity of each year from 1974 through 1983. The first was Richard Nixon. The last was Ronald Reagan. I would not choose either man as America's Sweetheart, but Nixon achieved his apotheosis through dedicated scrabbling, hard-earned governmental expertise, and profound character flaws. Reagan is a kind of logo, who knows as much about how the nation or the world functions as Betty Crocker knows about baking.

And yet Reagan works, in the thespian sense. He communicates serenity, because he isn't thoughtful enough to have any shame. He believes in his good-guy role, so why should he question himself? He was not ruffled when he called his own dog by the wrong name in front of the dog and reporters. That is what I call your definitive tinsel figure: a person who feels that he can afford, psychologically, not to know his own dog. Eventually such a person reveals greater gaps in his knowledge. He feels safe in assuming, for instance, that the Nazi Holocaust has pretty much blown over.

Yet Ronald Reagan represents abiding values to millions of people. He shrugs and grins and doesn't put himself out, and he is the most powerful man in the world. He *must have* paid his dues, because there he is. I would call it voodoo ascendancy, except that voodoo *gets down*. Celebrities today just loom large, like parade floats.

And yet I think more and more people are asking, "Who do celebrities think they are, anyway?" Celebrities today seem monumentally richer and more familiar. You'd think that a celebrity would feel obliged to be amazing, or at least colorful, but too many of them are content with being sufficiently famous that they don't have to be interesting. So who needs them?

"What I want to know," says my friend Jim Seay, the poet, "is how come every day it says in the paper that today is Bill Bixby's birthday. Or Tom Jones's. Or Loni Anderson's. How come it never says today is my mother's birthday? Or one of my uncles'? Or — I've got sisters, too. How come it never says it's one of their birthdays? That's what I'm interested in. I don't *care* if it's Tom Jones's birthday."

Seay comes from a county in Mississippi where the paper will have a picture of Mrs. Rainie Hazelrigs, who has grown a particularly large vegetable, and another one of Newland Fobes, who has killed three great big snakes. Mrs. Hazelrigs and Newland will be pointing to what they have grown or killed: the reasons for the pictures. Celebrities, to get their pictures in the paper, don't have to have done anything. They can just be standing there.

Today's celebrity is someone who has never allowed TV cameras into his home before, but he is making an exception this time, for "PM Magazine." Here's some good footage of him fixing himself a salad, just like a normal individual. Today's celebrity is someone who is a very private person, really, who is uncomfortable with all the glamour and acclaim. Prefers simple pleasures, like ironing. Any normal person who said he or she liked ironing would seem crazy. But celebrities get *credit* for liking to iron. I want you to read this from a recent story about Jackie Onassis in *People:*

> She eschews bodyguards and entourages and sometimes travels alone on Doubleday business. "I walk fast," Jackie explained. On a trip to Paris, she registered at the Hotel Crillon as "Mrs. Lancaster." She met photographer Deborah Turbeville for a tour of the dusty back rooms at Versailles, which Turbeville later photographed for the 1981 book *Unseen Versailles.* "One time she leaned out of the limo window to ask directions," says Turbeville. "She didn't cringe in the

car, making a big deal about it, like 'No one should see me, I'm Jacqueline Onassis.' "

Well, hell, most people would feel unreasonably privileged to be able to afford to register at the Hotel Crillon as anybody. Most people eschew bodyguards and entourages without even thinking about it, and not because bodyguards and entourages don't walk fast enough for them, either. Personally, if I had an entourage, I'd say, "Listen, y'all, I'm going to pick up the pace now," and if they couldn't keep up, I'd find me an entourage that could.

Now, I will say this: the way *People* puts it, it sounds as if Jackie Onassis *toured through the palace of Versailles in a limousine*. If she did, well, okay, that is interesting. My hat is off to anybody who would ride in an automobile of any kind right up the steps into a palace. My friends Slick Lawson, Susan Scott, and Greg Jaynes and I never did that, but we did close the castle of Versailles one night. We lurked around, hoping we'd get locked in, so we could sleep over in Marie Antoinette's bed. That wouldn't have been as interesting as tooling down the back halls in a big old long black car, but it would have been worth telling about if we'd managed to do it. But some Frenchmen made a sweep through the castle before locking up, and they made us leave.

I don't think Mrs. Onassis actually got limoed from room to room at Versailles, though (saying, "Driver, that looks like an interesting torture chamber; pull over there"). I think what *People* means is that Jackie Onassis stuck her head out of a limo and asked how to get to Versailles. Actually, as I remember, the roads are pretty well marked. In fact, the way the franc is now, it's a surprisingly cheap cab ride from Paris to Versailles. I know because Slick, Susan, Greg, and I missed the tour bus that night and took a cab back. I think it was just about twenty dollars, which split four ways is not bad at all. But nobody saw fit to write us up for getting a good deal like that. I have mentioned it myself a number of times, because I welcome the opportunity to let people know that I've been to France. Because it gives me a feeling of being snazzy. And people realize that I am trying to get them to help me feel snazzy, so they don't look impressed. A celebrity, though, can stick her head out of a limo in France and people will rush to regard it as just-an-ordinary-Joe behavior, which is to say, another star in her crown.

Incidentally, according to *People*, Jackie Onassis recently "scored a major publishing coup by signing up Michael Jackson to write his memoirs."

Jackie K. Onassis signs Michael "Beat It" Jackson. All right! We're talking *elements*. That's like the Hydrogen Sisters' getting on the horn to Dr. Oxygen and saying, "Let's make water." The only thing is, do you think there is an actual book here? I mean even an actual nonbook? And if there is, do you think Michael Jackson is going to write it? I believe he could *sing and dance* his memoirs, and I would pay to see him do it, but I don't see how it could take him very long. How old is he, nine? Even if he were Joan Collins's age, I have an inkling he would be, as a memoirist, no Joan Collins.

Of course, I've heard of celebrities, in the sports world, who never even read their autobiographies. Just went over the pictures carefully. I talked to somebody the other day who had talked to a photographer who had taken pictures of Michael Jackson. The photographer had wondered what Michael Jackson would be like, between pictures. He reported that between pictures, Michael Jackson just stood there, with one glove on.

Which is fine with me. Michael Jackson puts out when he's on-camera and keeps to himself when he's off. That's the way an icon ought to be. I don't want him telling us what he's really like. The next thing you know, Jackie Onassis will be signing up the Mona Lisa to write her memoirs. "I remember one day Da Vinch — I called him Leo Da Vinch, we would kid like that, he was just really very mellow — said to me, 'M.L. . . .' "

Can you believe there is a TV show called "Lifestyles of the Rich and Famous?" Actually, the life-style of the rich and famous consists of appearing as themselves on television. When they aren't appearing on "Lifestyles of the Rich and Famous," they are appearing on "$25,000 Pyramid" or "Celebrity Hot Potato." Can you believe there's a game show called "Celebrity Hot Potato?" Lainie Kazan and Jan Murray were scheduled recently. I have never watched "Lifestyles of the Rich and Famous," but I know what the celebrities do on it. They talk about how busy they are (busy appearing on shows like "Lifestyles of the Rich and Famous"), so busy they hardly have time to just kick off their shoes and throw a couple of mahogany table legs on the fire, or maybe a couple of bodyguards, and relax like everybody else.

I think celebrities ought to have second thoughts about trying to make a virtue out of being like everybody else. Celebrities can lose their sheen, just like everybody else. Recently, I heard about a guy who got thrown into the drunk tank and tried to get out by exclaiming loudly that he played guitar with a big country-music star, which was true.

Finally, he got somebody's attention. A jailer went back and looked at him through the bars and said, "You really play guitar with Doowayna Wheatstraw [not her real name]?"

"Yep," said the guy.

The jailer looked at him for a minute. "I fucked her maid," the jailer said, and then he walked away.

Only Hugh

OUT of 104 people in town here, just one's not famous: Hugh Odge.

Hugh says he doesn't mind; he says he wouldn't want the life of a Michael Johnson.

"Of a who?" we ask.

"You know. The one they set fire to. Radio musician."

"Jackson?"

"No, I know it's Michael something."

"Michael Jackson."

"I wouldn't want all the screaming."

Hugh, he's something. Just takes not being famous in his stride. *People* magazine was going to do a story about Hugh: "One in a Hundred — A Town's Sole Non-Celeb Knows Who He Is." But Hugh said no, he wouldn't be interviewed.

Different ones are famous for different things. Ordway Peary, you know, the ball lightning picked him up and flung him through a window of First Redeemed Church into Bethany Sweal's open coffin while she was being funeralized, which of course made her famous, too, but she didn't get any chance to enjoy it, even though Ordway startled her out of what it transpired must've been just a catalytic state, I think they said it was. They never did find out how she got into it.

But even though Ordway startled her out of it, well, put yourself in her shoes. When she came to, in a casket with a man who looked familiar but was sooty all over and had his clothes, eyebrows, and hair singed off and little bits of stained glass and lilies stuck to him, why she had a heart attack and died. Bethany, you know, never married.

Ginger Creekmore, last year when she was nine, was the one wrote a letter to the President saying she knew he had the interests of the Free World at heart in some cute way. I forget how she worded it, but he read it out loud on national TV and praised her by name, and then she got interviewed and said she wanted to grow up and be the person who operates the electric chair someday, so I guess the press had a heyday with that. You know how the press will do.

Mavis Dews, she was on "$25,000 Pyramid" with that one that plays the secretary on Bob Newhart, used to. When he was the psychopath. Now I guess he runs a hotel. Mavis said "Bosoms" as the answer to two different questions, I forget what the questions were, and it went over right well.

Talk about psychopaths, Vaughn and Marge Ogle actually had to start seeing one, they got so famous. They had some kind of marriage, I forget what it was called exactly, but it involved their birds some kind of way. It was quite the news when it came out on Charles Kuralt. Had parrots and, oh, cockertoos, cockerteels, all these different cockerbirds, and they would communicate through them, see, and started offering courses in it. But then so many people, instead of writing in, just showed up in their cars looking for personal counseling, *honking,* at all hours. It put so much pressure on Vaughn and Marge's marriage — well, they weren't married, for one thing. That came out. When they went on Donahue. Marge blurted that they weren't even interested in each other, hardly. They just both liked birds. She said the birds weren't all that interested in Vaughn, either, because he yelled and was too picky. Vaughn got all upset and said she was always trying to turn the birds against him.

Then come to find out Miz Wygrand was a folk artist, with her little figurines she makes with lard and putty and beef gristle and blow-in cards. Those are the little subscription cards that drop out of magazines all the time. She don't *take* any magazines, either — except, well, now *Art in America* ever since she was in it. But she always just hung around the post office and picked up the cards, and we always thought — well, we'd say, "She's harmless." Now they've got her in a museum in Toronto.

Earl and Ora Whisenant, they're the ones had the tag sale where somebody bought as a Eugyptian mummy what turned out — no, I guess it was the other way around. It was *sold* as a bundle of antique shirtwaists. And then later it was appraised as a Eugyptian mummy. Had just been down in their basement, all these years. Off in a corner.

So of course anyway we have a local roast every week. "We all knew Terrine before she was famous and I want to say she hasn't changed a bit. Course I don't know why she had to go and have a phone put in just so she could then turn around and unlist it."

She did, too. Terrine Pharr. She's the one — you must've seen her getting worked over by Ted Koppel — the one that adopted her father, changed his name legally, and then married him. You'd have to know Terrine; it wasn't anything like it looked. She just loves going through channels. Soon as she got it into her head that a private citizen could file a writ and all, why it was Katy bar the door. She had her dad incorporated, too, and registered as a flag of convenience. She sat next to Hugh Odge at one roast and he said, "Just don't declare me a national monument or nothing, Terrine, 'cause I don't want to be always shooing squirrels off my head."

Ed Liveright, now . . . What is it again that Ed is famous for? I believe it was *Ed* that was sold, *as* the Eugyptian mummy. No, because he won't go in anybody's basement. He's got a fear of depths.

* * *

I declare, it's getting hard to keep people straight. I used to know everybody in town and didn't have a second thought about it, but now that you've seen so many of them on TV, why I'll see somebody I've known for thirty years and say to myself, "Isn't that . . . ?" You know. I don't remember whether I know them or just know who they are. If you was to run Claus V. Bulow past me right now I'd have to stop and think whether I know him from seeing him on Merv or from having him sell me Red Wing shoes in specially narrow sizes out of his house. I have the narrowest feet, for a heavy-set man; my whole family do.

And Worley Belt, he does quite a business in outsizes with those Red Wings. He doesn't look anything like Claus Bulow; I'm just using him as an illustration of how you'll get confused. Worley's not famed for his shoes. He was on "20/20" concerning his own German dirigible that he was constructing off to one side of his house. Course we had to zone him out of that. Took it up before the commission, zoned him out of any lighter-than-air construction on his property. Hate to zone a man's land out of anything, but Worley wouldn't use helium, like normal people, he had to use hydrogen, for historical accuracy. And us sitting there in the shadow of it trying on shoes. We let him inflate it that one time, for the show, and be John Brown if it didn't blow sky-high. Great TV, oh, yeah. "But Worley," we said, "something like that is great TV *once.*"

At the roasts, though — matter of fact, we roasted Hugh Odge one time. Forgot he wasn't famous. He went along with it. Just requested no remarks about his baldness. We go through the jury rolls alphabetically — well, reverse-alpha-betically, because Fielder Yerkes is so old we wanted to make sure we got him in. It's his house, you know, where the face of Gene Rayburn showed up in the wood grain when he sanded down his porch door.

We don't roast Ordway Peary, because he don't want to hear about anything hot. Since the lightning. He was the one, remember, I told you was flung by the lightning? Into Bethany Sweal's arms? That's how they knew for sure she must've been brought back to life, because they had to prize him out of her grasp. Though I think frankly Ordway trades on his fame. Without bragging about it in detail, cause then he'd have to talk about the lightning. He don't want any mention of anything bright *or* hot. Course he will say *that* quite often.

You'll say something about the shooting stars being so bad this year and Ordway'll say, "Whoa. I'm going to have to ask you to change the topic. I don't want to hear *nothing* about anything that bright and hot." And he'll look off into the distance. Ordway I think is one person who it went to his head.

The rest of us take it right well, don't make a big deal of it, you know. We have a celebrity picnic every year; Hugh Odge gets to come as somebody's guest. And he will, too; he's used to being around us — you know, he doesn't feel like he's got to be pointing people out. Ordway, now, he'll get kind of obvious about standing a long way from where the wienies are being cooked.

Ordway, of course, he was one of the most dead-set ones of us against Worley Belt's zeppelin. Ordway'd go from house to house and wouldn't even say, "After all I've been through." He'd just look off into the distance and say he felt it especially incumbent on him to raise certain issues.

That's something a lot of us have wrestled with — whether we ought to speak out, you know, on things like, oh, crises of the world. Just because a man's got national attention for being glued to the floor of his rocks-gems-and-minerals shop by holdup men — taking Kaymore Dark for example. They used that Super Glue, you know, he like to never got up *off* that floor; he did three interviews while he was stuck there. Just because a man's a household name for being glued to his floor or whatever, don't by virtue of that make him an expert on the deficit, say.

But some of us feel like, well, maybe we have a responsibility to speak out when it's something that affects every generation. Earl Whisenant started a petition to outlaw social studies in the nation's schools. I didn't sign it, because I didn't think I ought to influence people to say to themselves, "Well, he's on TV," just because I'm on TV, "I guess I ought to sign too." It's something I've thought a lot about.

How I got my show was, the cable was out here filming a movie based on one of us, I forget which one, and the producer, Barry, and I got talking. He said he was looking for fresh faces, people that hadn't been in whitener commercials or on "The Salt of the Earth Show" or anything. And I hadn't. And his eyes lit up, because, the way he put it, "The thing is, you *look* like you haven't."

So, well, I guess they built the whole concept around me. "Nobody Special." I'm the host, and our staff goes far and wide to find guests that maybe aren't fabulous, maybe didn't ever do anything all that incredible, maybe wouldn't ever be picked out of a crowd, but that's the point. People are getting back to the basic values now. People want to know there are average people out there: it's reassuring. People look at our show and say, "What business has *that* character got being on TV?" And seems like it gives them a lift.

And, of course, well, it's made a difference in my life. I can pick up *Us* magazine and feel like a part of it now. I tried to get Hugh Odge to do a spot on the show, but he said, "No, I just couldn't handle the pulling on my coattails. Everybody getting my reaction to this, that, and the other. Breaking into my trailer home wanting to know what I'm really like."

Then too there are some in town who maintain Hugh isn't doing anything more in this world than just biding his time. Particularly since he started building that — well, to hear Hugh tell it, he's not building anything, he's just puttering. We don't really know what it is. But it's taking shape. And the zoning commission's getting concerned. "If you ask me," Worley Belt was saying the other day, "it's a ark."

Can Carl Lewis Be Repackaged?

IT is not my place, as a slow white person with mongrel dogs and a Plymouth Horizon, to tell a supersonic black person with a virgin-white Samoyed and a BMW how to repackage himself. But I am going to. Everyone else may be willing to let the world's most famous active athlete go on being eerily boring, but I think the man has *potential*.

How anybody who always does exactly what he is of a mind to, and who moves like the Greek god of Thrust conjoint with the Greek god of Flow, and who operates like the California god of Public Relations, can have managed to win four gold medals, find opulence through amateurism, appear on the cover of *Time* twice in three weeks, and still lay an egg, I don't know. But that is the feat Carl Lewis pulled off at the 1984 Olympics.

He came in image-heavy. It is said that the mother of Peisidorous, an ancient Olympic boxing champion, disguised herself as a man so that she could act as her son's second. Then when he won she forgot herself, took him into her arms, and caressed him. This incident led to a rule requiring all Olympic trainers to appear naked, which I imagine did not make Peisidorous the sentimental favorite four years later. I can see them now, a chorus of little gnarled guys from the Hellenic equivalent of Canarsie, chewing on the Hellenic equivalent of unlit cigars and cracking:

> Woe! Thou best had show us something now,
> For 'tis thy mama's fault, behold, alas:
> We here must with our balls out hanging stand.

But at least Peisidorous did not come into the Olympics with a penchant for wearing, at various times, pointed white-rim glasses, orange-and-black harlequin tights, eyebrow pencil, orange lip-gloss, and a haircut that made him look unsettlingly like the metasexual New Wave *poseuse* and singer Grace Jones. Nor did Peisodorous have a manager who said things like "No one's ever had a Carl Lewis going into the Olympics before. We're on the frontier," and "We want Carl to be identified with one major company, the way O. J. Simpson is with Hertz or Bob Hope is with Texaco."

Peisidorous was not threatening to sue some Italians who planned to film a documentary on him. Carl Lewis was. "I don't want to be diluted," he told Gary Smith of *Sports Illustrated.*

The Lewises are a tight family, who do not see themselves in terms of "people." Said Carl's long-jumping sister Carol: "People aren't what they wish they were — and we are." As it turned out in Los Angeles, Carol finished behind quite a few people, and showed dissatisfaction with herself. Tell us about it, Carol. Welcome to life. But Carl — who says things like "failure doesn't loom in me" — won all the golds he'd set for himself, and demonstrated great galloping self-pleasure before an audience of millions and millions. I suggest, however, that quite a few of those watchers were saying, "Carl, take a flying leap."

It was in the long jump that Carl Lewis stepped on his dick. After leaping far enough to win the gold, he played it safe. Three times his turn came around for another shot at Bob Beamon's epochal world and Olympic record, but each time, as the global village cut away from whatever else it was doing to focus on Carl Lewis alone, he passed. He saved his energy for the other events he had to win in order to pre- serve his appeal as a corporate front-person. Judicious busi- ness strategy, perhaps. But celestial athletes do not become American heroes by keeping their powder and lip-gloss dry. (Especially when, right after the next commercial, tiny scarcely ripened gymnast women are busting their humps as if in one last desperate effort to forestall Armageddon.) As of this writing, no major U.S. corporation has leapt to embrace a harlequin-panted jock who is such a hotshot he doesn't need heroic.

So it's repackaging time. Lewis and his manager led up to the Olympics with a four-year, six-point promotional plan. I propose these six new points for a Great Leap Forward:

1. Marry the daughter of the chairman of the board of a major company. Or his son.

Carl Lewis's sexuality, of course, is none of our business. Sure. Here we have a man who carries his own TV makeup kit, displays his buns in *Vanity Fair,* collects china and crys- tal, wears puffed-sleeve jackets, and on the other hand drives 125 miles an hour with a Fuzzbuster in his car and says, "If you are very masculine and believe in yourself, it is very hard to attack your masculinity." A lot of people want to know who a guy like that is taking to the dance.

And all he will tell us is, "I could be sleeping with a horse for all [people] know," and "It's not as though six people have caught me in bed with six men." Most of the characters John Wayne played could have said the former and Truman Capote could have said the latter. Do we want a vigorous twenty-one-year-old American hero who either never has sex or never has it with anybody he wants to be seen with? True, Michael Jackson seems to get away with one or the other, but (a) he is a Jehovah's Witness and (b) an element of creepiness works in rock and roll. As opposed to track and field.

What if Lewis's sexuality is something major companies

and Mr. and Mrs. America frown on? Well, every American hero's sexuality must include a broad streak of philosophy summarizable as follows: "Fuck 'em." Otherwise, how are major companies and Mr. and Mrs. America going to learn anything?

2. Revive redneck chic.

Joe Namath worked against type by making panty-hose commercials. Carl Lewis might start saying things like "all vines and no taters." Fortunately there is a sound new book out, *You All Spoken Here,* by Roy Wilder, Jr., which provides any number of useful expressions: "He lies so bad he hires somebody to call his dogs." "He's so tight, when he grins his pecker skins back." "He's been places and et in hotels." "Fast as salts in a widder woman." "Dumber than a barrel of hair."

3. Start hanging out with somebody other than family or walk-around guys.

How about Chuck Yeager. Vanessa Williams. Geraldine Ferraro. George Burns. It would humanize Carl Lewis's profile if people were to ask George Burns what the two of them did together and Burns were to reply, "He wanted me to run with him but when we came to the first lap I sat in it. Then I introduced myself and she said, 'Aren't you going to go any farther?' I said, 'It's nice of you, but not at my age.' She said, 'Aren't you going to jump with Carl?' I said, 'No. At my age, what could surprise me that much?' "

4. Collect something different.

I have been told that Waterford crystal fits into a new mandarin elegance among rich black males. Well. Maybe. I still say it sucks. He who accumulates crystal is bound to start watching his step. Remember when someone broke into Carl Lewis's house during the Olympics and smashed all his crystal? That might not have happened if he'd collected something more people could identify with, like duck decoys.

5. Develop vulnerability.

Carl Lewis insists on being a master of all he deigns to touch. "He is secure enough to *risk*," says his acting coach.

But there is actors' vulnerability, and then there is folks' vulnerability. A real American hero — Muhammad Ali, Richard Pryor, Billie Jean King — is out-of-plumb enough to keep his security hopping. Who wants a hero who is all ups and no downs? For starters, Carl Lewis could go fishing on "The American Sportsman" and — no, not fall in. Just not catch anything.

6. *Do something for free.*

After the Olympics, Lewis's agent claimed that his client had turned down $100,000 for a single track meet and would not sign with a pro football team for less than $1 million a year. Since Lewis is said to hate the macho regimentation of football (hey, I too would rather watch "Kate and Allie" and "Cagney and Lacey" than "Monday Night Football"), this means that he would undertake half a year of something he can't stand for seven figures, but wouldn't do one night of something he loves for six. This is not heroic. Far better would be for Carl Lewis to give himself over to some large-scale charity effort. This would prove he is rich. It also might do Carl Lewis *and* people some good.

How about a Carl Lewis Telethon? To combat a major affliction. I have one in mind. It strikes hundreds of thousands of contemporary Americans: lawyers, bishops, campaign aides, yuppies, consultants, TV Christians, Pentagon officials, and, yes, superstar athletes. I don't know the scientific name for this condition, but down home we used to call it Too Stuffed to Jump.

Who You Gonna Call?

Ever since John Wayne became a ghost, America has been yearning for a real guy. "Who you gonna call?" asks the theme song of *Ghostbusters*, the most copiously grossing movie of 1984.

Are you gonna call Clint Eastwood? No, he gets off on wasting punks. Burt Reynolds? No, he has gone too arch. Ronald Reagan? Well, the electorate certainly clings to him; wants to believe he is a real guy.

Bill Murray, the star of *Ghostbusters*, is one. It is as if the usher, after unsolicitously lighting you to your seat, has walked on down the aisle and stepped onto the screen. And done a take and looked back in your general direction and said, "Catch this action."

Murray never quite seems to be in the right place, and yet there he is, enjoying it. "I was going to go into the army and train to be a doctor," he says, "but my friends were going to college so I went to Regis, this Jesuit school in Colorado. I arrived with my first Dopp kit and everything. They said, 'You never answered when we accepted you. We don't have a place for you.' So I stayed in the lobby of the dorm, over where they kept the coats, until some guy quit. People would ask me what room I was in. I'd point to the coats and say, 'Ohh, over there. . . .' "

Today, it is true, Murray has a big penthouse on Manhattan's ritzy East Side. But it is also true that he says to his doorman, "Hey, great shoes. You make those in prison?" True, *Ghostbusters* is said to have earned him, personally, something in the low eight figures. True, Murray can now get away with just about anything in Hollywood — even portraying, in *The Razor's Edge,* a spiritually enlightened person. But that doesn't mean he is going la-di-da on us.

Of course there are people to whom this does not seem to be the issue. There are people who feel Murray is not la-di-da enough.

"Murray?" these people will say. "I saw him at the Olympics closing ceremony. He and this TV cameraman were shoving each other."

"Murray? I saw him at a big Oscars party. Everybody's in a tux except Murray, who's in jeans and a T-shirt and looks drunk."

I remember being at a Super Bowl several years ago, doing my best to act childish throughout Pasadena and its environs, and hearing the rumor that Murray and Hunter Thompson had just peed on the rug in the lobby of the Beverly Hills Hotel. I remember thinking, Well, I can't keep up with that action. I can respect it. I can see the point of it. But I just can't keep up with it.

I have known Murray since before he was famous, but I'd never sat down with him and said, "Billy, you maniac, what are you *up* to?" Now I have. And I think he is keeping a flame alive. True, the amounts of money he is making are obscene enough to establish him solidly in the eighties. But as long as he is wrestling ghosts, looking scruffy, and keeping an eye cocked for the meaning of life, the sixties are not dead.

Like all the guys he has played onscreen, from demented greenkeeper to seeker after higher truth, Murray is a great kidder. And I mean that sincerely. The son of a bitch can kid. I have watched him kid Yogi Berra, my children, John

Candy, some Himalayan village women (onscreen in *The Razor's Edge,* but you could tell they were real Himalayan village women and he was really kidding with them), a Guatemalan waiter, even autograph seekers.

It takes grace to kid autograph seekers, since they are always running after you in the street. But I watched Murray deal with them as if he and they were all in the street together.

"Will you sign this 'To John'?" asked a panting man in his thirties.

"John," said Murray, signing, "what the fuck kind of name is *John?"*

"Would you sign this for my sister, she's a real diehard," asked a college-age youth waving what looked like half a McDonald's napkin.

"Try hitting her when she's sleeping," counseled Murray as he signed. "Wait till she dozes off, and . . . "

Then there was a guy who looked to be in his twenties and confessed to being in insurance who came up to Murray and John Candy on Fifty-fourth Street and Fifth Avenue in Manhattan and said, "You got to breakdance with me. I got to tell people I was breakdancing with Bill Murray and John Candy." So the guy lay down on his back on the sidewalk in his business shirt and tie, and Murray and Candy each got him by a leg; first they had him going in two different directions, but then they got together and spun him around. And he appreciated it. It was kind of nice. Murray and Candy didn't have anything better to do, and it meant a lot to the guy.

As people go, famous actors don't have the highest reputation for being exactly *there* in real life. Murray does have a way of disappearing, but often it is *into* real life. During the period when I was plumbing him for this portrait he was off unreachable somewhere in San Francisco for a couple of weeks. But then he resurfaced, as he said he would, and it turned out he had been helping a friend stucco two houses.

There he was, an idol of millions, all nicked up from the chicken wire you use to hold wet stucco on a wall. To be recognized less, he had altered his appearance. The last time I'd seen him he looked like Professor Irwin Corey. Now he had let his beard grow so that he looked like a young Karl Marx or a reflective Yosemite Sam. Or Professor Irwin Corey with a big beard.

In his efforts to eschew false glamour, Murray has at least one thing working for him: the more he needs a haircut, the more he looks like Professor Irwin Corey. And yet onscreen he is the joint reincarnation of Harpo Marx and Clark Gable. We do not think characters played by beautiful actresses are crazy when they go for him, nor do we doubt it when characters played by people like Dustin Hoffman think he is cool. We wonder, if we let ourselves go a little seedier and stopped holding our stomachs in (Murray looks vaguely athletic, but his midsection and Richard Gere's do not seem to belong to the same period in history), whether we might be in better touch with ourselves, or even with characters played by beautiful actresses.

I like the way he runs in *Ghostbusters*. He is never quite as comic a mover as a Marx brother; he seems like a real guy running. But if a gait can roll its eyes slightly, that is what Murray's gait does. He seems to be sharing a small joke with his body.

Sometimes in movies he doesn't seem to be doing much of anything. I have never seen a performance quite like his in *Tootsie*. There he is in the middle of a tightly organized, concept-centered movie, playing the soft-edged buddy of the intensely focused Dustin Hoffman. All he does is sit around musing, off in his own world, occasionally saying things like "I think we're getting in a weird area here," and he gives the movie a kind of second focus that mocks the concept (the way Abbie Hoffman made fun of America) yet makes it more convincing.

Murray did not develop this knack overnight. He grew up

in a big, economically marginal Catholic family, in a mostly affluent neighborhood outside Chicago, competing for laughs at the dinner table with his eight siblings and never dreaming of becoming an actor. After either dropping out or being kicked out of everything from Boy Scouts to college, he drifted into Old Town, where Chicago's hippies hung out, and followed his older brother Brian Doyle-Murray into Second City, the comedy-theater group that produced most of "Saturday Night Live"'s early stars. His first experience at Second City was an improvisation class. "I was so bad!" he says. But later he ran into a director of the troupe who said she would give him a scholarship if he would paint her kitchen purple. "It was one of the biggest shit jobs I ever did," he says. "There were all these ceiling pipes that had to be purple.

"Second City was a great life," he recalls. "Waking up at eight-thirty at night, drinking free at the theater. But it was tough starting out. Nobody would want to work with you. You weren't any good, for one thing. But how were you going to learn? John Candy and I went through hell together. He and I did fifty of the worst improvisations anybody ever saw. If you got any kind of laugh, they'd bring the lights down, just so you could have some kind of ending. Afterward, you'd be screaming backstage — the audience would hear you screaming and crying. Then you'd walk off into the night. That's *really* not getting your rocks off."

But Murray eventually improved, and five years later graduated to "Saturday Night Live," where no one could ever find him. Most of the cast lived the show and breathed the show — slept in the studio or with a phone right next to the pillow in case of a middle-of-the-night call to confer on a sketch revision. Murray was always late or missing; he'd show up for read-throughs with ideas that he hadn't thoroughly worked out, much less typed up. And whatever people wrote for him he would rewrite. It appeared for a while, after he joined the show as Chevy Chase's replacement in 1977, that he wouldn't last. But his oily lounge singer and his cozy-with-the-giants entertainment reporter and his beltline-above-the-stomach nerd won their way into late-night Americans' skewed hearts. And now, of all "Saturday Night Live"'s early stars, he is the only one to establish himself resoundingly, by critical and financial standards, in the movies.

Alan Zweibel, who wrote for "SNL" in its glory days, says that most of the people on the show were so devoted to producer Lorne Michaels and his vision that he could understand how a Reverend Jim Jones could arise. But Murray, Zweibel says, always kept a distance — was part of the gang but had his own notions. Now he is doing more to perpetuate the show's tradition than anybody else. At John Belushi's funeral, Murray and Dan Aykroyd got together and, Murray says, "we said we went through something together on that show that no one who wasn't on it could understand. And we shouldn't let it be lost."

The show had great outrage and liberation. It also had nihilism. It was making great television by trashing television. When Belushi and Aykroyd made movies that trashed movies — *1941, The Blues Brothers* — the effect was less felicitous. And then Belushi trashed himself. Murray, meanwhile, gained more and more clout in godless Hollywood by playing these laid-back guys who seem to be watching the movie right alongside the audience and yet are running around in the midst of the movie having a good time and making the whole enterprise seem friendly. "Lorne always talks about the danger in Murray's eyes when he's performing," says Zweibel. "But the truth is, there's always something there that says, however wild I get, you're safe with me."

When you're with him, Murray can suddenly leave the room mentally on you. But here's what I think he is doing, and I wouldn't say this about every actor: I think he is thinking.

Because Murray does not kid constantly. He is unlike "Saturday Night Live" in that not everything is tongue-in-cheek with him. For instance, we were at the Hard Rock Café in New York, which is part-owned by Aykroyd and is where Murray's brother John is a bartender. We were drinking and staying up all night and kidding around with NBC sports commentator Ahmad Rashad and an MTV tape jockey and this guy Alex Hodges I went to high school with, who went on to become Otis Redding's agent. I noticed that over the dance floor were these enormous letters that said ALL IS ONE.

And I said, "Why'd they put *that* there?" (Because, hey, I come out of the fifties. I do not know from mysticism other than Methodist hymns. And when I stay out late in New York, it is not so I can be informed that all is one. It is so I won't meet any other Methodists.)

But Murray's answer was, "I guess because they believe it."

I think Murray goes over so well as the questionable exorcist in *Ghostbusters,* as the dry roomie in *Tootsie,* as the goof-off with leadership qualities in *Stripes,* partly because he is a great kidder and partly because he conveys this sense that if cinematic comedy doesn't work out, there are other realms. "Anybody can get a laugh," he says. "I'm interested in making sense."

Offscreen, Murray is the kind of guy who finds places like Kelley's. Kelley's, which is in the middle of Miami somewhere, is the best bar you have ever been in unless you are exclusively into luxe. I heard that Kelley's burned down last year, at least to its walls and ceiling, but that it is still in business. I haven't checked it out yet, but I know that Kelley's is not the kind of place that fire would hamper much.

Kelley's opens out onto the street (I mean it did even before it burned down, if indeed it has burned down) so that you have plenty of room to dance to the jukebox, which has everything you want, including "Good Night, Irene." That's the biggest song at Kelley's; when it comes on, everyone present sings it, and an elderly woman at the end of the bar beats the hell out of this bell on the wall, and everyone else grabs up these cans full of popcorn kernels and bangs them on the bar. . . .

You probably have to be there. Murray talked Jimmy Buffett into going there once, and they sat around and sat around and nothing went on and Buffett was saying he had to get somewhere and then suddenly somebody drove a Fiat right up almost *into* Kelley's and people piled out of it, and the lady who sits at the end of the bar arrived, and there were so many renditions of "Good Night, Irene" that everybody lost count.

"I love Miami," Murray says. "People there really keep track of their personal freedom. There are so many old people . . . they don't want anybody giving them any shit. And you don't have many laws down there. I met some third-generation smugglers whose family had been cutting deals with the Indians before Florida was even a state."

In New York, Murray found this great Japanese piano bar, and another place that sometimes serves "inverted margaritas" — they put a funnel in your mouth and pour in the ingredients. I met a guy in the second place one night who told me he invented those little computer lines they put on everything you buy now and that he had twelve bidets in his apartment. I asked what he needed twelve bidets for. He said, "I might get lucky."

Time, Newsweek, and *People* all wanted to do cover stories on Murray when *Ghostbusters* became a hit, but he wouldn't cooperate. It is his feeling that "those magazines take your picture and they make up their minds who you are from that picture and they base the story on that, and millions of people see it, and from then on, that's *you.* It sucks the soul out of you."

Murray is not kidding about that. Nor is he taking lightly the perils of Hollywood. "I'm on all these mailing lists now.

An invitation a week to all these charity events. They want you to be on the dais or the committee — which is ten famous actors, ten people you never heard of, and fifty of the biggest criminals in the world. And it's a benefit for wounded babies." Third-generation smugglers are one thing, but Hollywood biggies are another. "They're on all these decency committees. And they are the biggest thieves and crooks in the world.

"Sometimes I feel like they are really running everything and I'm kidding myself. You know the original idea of fear and loathing — it's figuring out the worst thing that could happen in a situation and being ready for it. As an exercise, it prepares you for Hollywood. Hollywood has the same power over you that the FBI does, or the CIA. Look what they did to Preston Sturges — they thought he was too big and they broke him. I don't know why. It could happen to anybody."

It was happening to Belushi when he died. It's not happening to Murray. He says he has improvised, written, or reworked almost all the lines he has delivered in movies. He refuses to have an answering service so he can avoid people ("You can continue to change your number, or you can not answer the phone, or you can answer the phone in Swedish"). He has made millions and not spent many of them (no drug problems, for one thing). Money, as such, doesn't mean much to him. "When I really get *down,*" he says, "and I'm walking around in the street and really pissed, I think, At least I'm rich. But that's really grasping at straws." He can, however, afford to be choosy about projects. He agreed to do *Ghostbusters* for Columbia only if they would let him and his friend, director John Byrum, do *The Razor's Edge* (for which Murray took only a fee for cowriting the screenplay).

The two of them wrote the movie all over the world, from the Frank Sinatra Room of the Friars Club to a curbstone in Paris, by way of the Himalayas. (Murray has a good-looking, responsible and highly understanding wife, Mickey, and a two-

and-a-half-year-old chunk of energetic son, Homer, but he gets to roam the globe. And he gets to name his son Homer Banks William Murray, for Ernie Banks, who hit homers. Murray is a Cubs fan. His mother made him stick in the William so she can call the kid "little Billy.") Originally a W. Somerset Maugham novel, *The Razor's Edge* was first filmed in 1946, starring Tyrone Power as a man named Larry Darrell who goes around in remarkably high-waisted pants "searching for something. Something I can't put into words." There are exchanges like this:

"Have you found that peace of mind you were looking for?"

"No, but for the first time I'm beginning to see things in a clear light."

The Murray-Byrum version is more hip. It turns great kidding into a mode of spiritual enlightenment. The character as Murray plays him is different from everybody else, more engaging and yet less satisfied, by virtue of his sense of humor. It's a very interesting, personal yet cool, straight yet funny performance. In one scene, Piedmont, a character played by Brian Doyle-Murray, dies after saving Larry Darrell's life. In his grief, Darrell holds him in his arms and begins to recite all of Piedmont's *bad* qualities. "He really enjoyed disgusting people; the thrill of offending people and making them uncomfortable. He was despicable. I'll never understand gluttony, but I hate it. And I hated him. You," he says to Piedmont's body, "will not be missed."

Murray says he had his brother in mind during that scene, but also Belushi. After Belushi died Murray was with Aykroyd and some of Aykroyd's relatives. They were all sitting around in black silence. Murray recalled something he had read about the Sufi religion. Certain Sufis have a custom of recalling terrible things about the dearly departed. So Murray recited several terrible things that Belushi had done, and everybody in the room could think of several more, and soon everyone felt able to rise to the grim occasion.

I guess that's a form of kidding death, but a more highly evolved form of it than used to be practiced on "Saturday Night Live."

"The year Teddy Kennedy was running against Jimmy Carter," Murray recalls, "I saw a picture of Kennedy in the Saint Patrick's Day parade in Chicago. There he was, wearing a bulletproof vest. I don't know, I think I cried or something, it was just so sad. I felt terrible about it. I called Hunter Thompson and he got in touch with somebody and — actually, I just handed out things. Got in a cab and went out to Co-op City in the Bronx at eleven in the morning the day of the primary . . . everybody out there had already voted by then. But I figured, if this fucker is going out there with a bulletproof vest on, at least I can . . .

"And I had done him on 'Saturday Night Live' — low, cheap, Chappaquiddick stuff. Kept pulling seaweed out of my mouth. I'm not crazy about actors going public about politics. But down the road a way, something is going to have to happen.

"In *The Razor's Edge,* in the end, when I say I'm going back to America . . . *America* is sort of a word people use in the modern world to mean a place where there is real spiritual freedom. I have a feeling that what is wrong or right about the world is very clear and simple: No war. Don't kill Asians. Don't beat up on people who are smaller than you are. We go down to Grenada, where they had one revolution repulsed by a guy pointing an unloaded twenty-two at a boatload of people. It's like taking over a window-cleaning office in Manhattan. And people say, 'Now we can hold our heads high in the world.' " He shakes his head.

"There's a whole generation out there . . . everybody was pretty righteous from about eighteen till twenty-four, until they realized they had to make a buck. I wonder, where did all those people go? Where in the hell did they go? When John Lennon died, they came out again, for the first time in ten years. It was amazing, a lost race materialized. Somebody said they're like Zapata's army. A time's going to come, somewhere down the road."

So there is one rich thirty-five-year-old in the country who isn't a yuppie.

Murray and I were watching the Olympics on TV when the American men gymnasts beat the Chinese and then got ecstatic. "Those boys are *conscious* now," Murray said. "They won't be able to remember it tomorrow because they won't be conscious. But they'll remember it whenever they're conscious again.

"That's my technique now, I guess. It's hard to call it a technique when it's something much bigger. When the cameras roll, I think: This is the most important thing I'm going to do. It's going to be the biggest experience I'll ever share with other people. The biggest moment of contact with people right now. And if you're there, conscious of that . . . what you do doesn't look hard."

It is hard to talk about what an actor does, especially if, as Murray says, "the next day I act like a complete asshole and punch somebody in a bar. I'm still the same person, unfortunately. I'm not going to save the world because my own self is the first problem."

One reason Murray is engaging on the screen is that he lets his own self in on the joke. "Ah, yes," he seems to be saying, "here you are a movie star, running from a special effect." (As a matter of fact, he says, he is getting tired of making comedies "that end in an explosion.") He has been able to include America in that joke without losing himself in the process.

Maybe you would rather save the world by stockpiling bombs and invading Grenada. Murray prefers to make contact with potential enemies, himself included, by thinking on his feet and lightly evoking higher values.

He tells a story about driving around Chicago a few years ago, seven people in the car all smoking dope, and it's the first time he's been back in town since 1968, when the Old Town area was like an armed camp, cops milling around in wagons just waiting for someone to look halfway bustable.

"And all of a sudden we come to a stop right next to a paddy wagon. Inside are two of the biggest-headed guys I've ever seen. Just *huge*-headed guys. And we have really long hair.

"I'm driving. I don't want to sit still in the water for these guys, that is sure suicide. So I figure in these situations, if you can say something first . . . say, 'Excuse me. Can you tell me where the Claes Oldenburg baseball bat is?'

"He gets out of the paddy wagon. I say, 'We're fucked.'

"He comes to the window. He says, 'The Claes Oldenburg bat is in front of the Social Security Building. The Picasso woman is at the Civic Center. The Calder standing mobiles are at the Federal Center, and the Chagall mosaic mural is at the First National Bank.'

"I say, 'Thanks very much.'

"Cops in Chicago used to be so scary. I think those art pieces really changed that town. We did go to see that baseball bat, and it was everything I ever wanted it to be."

On Politics

If Joe McCarthy
Had been less swarthy,
And the other one, Gene,
Had been less clean . . .

Testimonial, Head-on

A ND now for a message that takes real courage:
I can't find it in my heart to like light beer. I would
rather have one heavy beer than seven light ones. I wouldn't
mind having seven heavy ones. And I don't really care what
brand the last four and a half of them are.

When I speak of courage I am not alluding to the risk of
corpulence on my part. I believe a person should live in such
a way that he can carry a little corpulence. The reason it
takes courage is this: I guess it rules out my appearing in a
great beer commercial.

I, a living American, accept that I will never be in a great
beer commercial, probably. With no less gravity would an
eighteenth-century Viennese have said to himself, "Let's
face it. You ain't ever going to hit a great lick on a clavier,
probably." Great beer commercials are so good they nearly
do a transcendant thing in our culture: they nearly redeem
television.

I don't mean the beer commercials with actors in them.
Those icky-yuppie figments of the "Tonight is kinda special" stripe are *not beery*. Nor can I tolerate that around-the-
campfire vignette in which one guy goes off into the woods
to talk a grizzly bear out of a case of Stroh's. Here we have a

workable concept, ruined by performances so callow that any half-grown bear, grizzly or fluffy, would chase those guys *and* their campfire all the way back to Hotchkiss.

I mean the beer commercials with real people in them: the Miller Lite ones with Bubba Smith, Boog Powell, Jim Honochick, John Madden, Marv Throneberry, Bob Uecker, and all. Those commercials are the only form of television that captures what jocks are like. (Which is to say, what everybody wants to be like when he or she is drinking beer.) They may be the only form of television that captures what *people* are like.

Most of the time as we watch television what are we thinking? "Unhhhhh. Television." Or, "Holy jumping . . . Great television! But should the children be witnessing actual dismemberment?" Or, "Will wonders never cease? Considering it's television, this almost bears some relation to art or life!"

Great beer commercials, however, are fresh, full-bodied, tasty: better than "MASH," for my money, and almost as good as "The Honeymooners." Being commercials, they are what television is all about; and yet there is actually something genuine about them. True, the point is to sell light beer by showing heavy guys drinking it. But these guys (who have lived in such a way that they can carry a little corpulence) are being funny about drinking beer *in ways that people actually are funny,* or think they are, *when they are drinking beer.*

Of course these heavy guys do not take any beer into their mouths, onscreen. And I know the poignance of that.

Years ago, after I wrote a book on the Steelers, I appeared in a commercial, shown in Pittsburgh, for Iron City beer. (This was back before there was light.) It wasn't a great commercial, because I was alone — didn't have Dick Butkus to bounce off of. But it was heartfelt, and it taught me how to execute "the beauty pour." The beauty pour means transferring beer from bottle to glass with so fine a touch that the suds rise just far enough above the brim; look irresistibly *heady;* but do not crest and break and come running down your arm.

The beauty pour does not, however, entail drinking any beer, aside from what you may be able to lick off your arm while the director isn't looking. I did thirty-eight takes of my commercial, and listened to thirty-eight beers being poured unaesthetically down the toilet, as I sat there feeling more and more porous and dry. Beer commercials waste more beer than Carrie Nation.

How would you like to film a love scene with a beautiful person of the diametrically opposite sex who is topped off by this wonderful pouf of hair that you can't wait to stick your nose into, and thirty-eight times — just when your lips are about to meet — have her snatched away, murdered, and replaced by someone else fully as comely and unattainable? I don't think I have been as drunk since, as I went out and got right after filming my beer commercial.

But you can tell that the people in the Miller Lite commercials have, in their time, swallowed a few. They are not getting all misty and warm over what a wonderful institution beer is for bringing the right sort of persons together. They are getting the way people get, ideally, when they are having fun drinking beer: rowdy without serious breakage, lightsome in a ponderous sort of way, and just confused enough to be entertaining.

Why aren't more commercials, for beer or anything else, as fitting as these? Why do so many of them involve, for instance, children beaming in ways that children never beam and exclaiming things that children never exclaim? "Gee, Mom, these Hodgson-Furbinger Reconstituted Thaw-'n'-Sizzle Fish Nuggets are really *something else.*"

If only I were able to believe, for thirty seconds, that light beer tastes like beer.

As Well As I Do My Own, Which Is What?

W HEN someone takes too authoritative a tone with my friend Slick Lawson, the Nashville photographer, he will say, "Well, I go along with what Donald Wilson Breland said about that."

Then he will proceed to snap pictures. After a few moments the person who has taken too authoritative a tone will say, "Well . . . I don't *know* Breland. Of course I know his *work*. . . ."

Then Slick will go on to mention that Donald Wilson Breland was a kid who sat in front of him in the fourth grade and ate paste. And what Donald Wilson Breland said, about everything, was "Whutcha wawnt *me* t' do uhbout it?"

Someone is going to catch me out like that someday. And only because I am trying to be gracious.

At my twenty-fifth high school reunion last year, you would have been proud of me. The way I called those names up, with seldom even a quick half-glance at a tag, you would have thought they were Ajax, Salome, Mrs. Miniver, and Jackie Robinson. I hadn't seen Steve Fladger or Mickey Wallis in a quarter of a century, and they were the only two returning members of the class whose bone structure had changed (late height spurts) since graduation. But their names came to me like the list of vowels; because I had learned them when I was fresh, back before I had met or heard of 375,000 other Americans. By the time anyone gets to be forty-three, if he has followed current events and been out of town a few times, two-thirds of the names he hears sound vaguely, but only vaguely, familiar.

People ask me, "Do you know Mason Swint?"

And I am not sure whether:

(a) I certainly do.

(b) I don't personally, but I do know *of* him, because he is the one who just won an Emmy or Oscar or Grammy or Tony or Obie or Golden Globe or Gold Glove or Olympic gold or Nobel or National Book Award or that other thing that's like the National Book Award or one of the three or four world junior light-heavyweight championships.

(c) I don't personally, but I do know *of* him, because he is that petting-zoo operator who was charged with lambkin, piglet, and duckling abuse.

(d) I am thinking of Morgan Swift, Morris Wilt, Milton Sweet, Marion Sweat, Morton Swing, Martin Short, or Myron Smart, some of whom I am sure I do know, or know of, and some of whom I believe I do, unless I am thinking of Mason Swint.

I should cut down on my name intake. But I don't want anyone to think that I don't know who's who in my field. And I don't know what my field is. Furthermore, I love names too much, for their own sake. How can I close my eyes to the fact that Stanford University has professors named Condoleezza Rice, an arms-control specialist, and Jon Roughgarden, an ecologist? All those *z*'s and *g*'s, on one faculty! Roughgarden should be a common term, like roughhouse or rough fish. Condoleezza Rice, according to the *Stanford Observer,* is from Birmingham, Alabama, and "her unusual name of Condoleezza is derived from the Italian musical term *con dolce* which means 'with sweetness.' " Ah.

Does Condoleezza rhyme with Louisa, pizza, mezza? In this country names can ring a range of bells. My friend Walter Iooss, the Flemish-American sports photographer, pronounces his name like "Yost" only with another *s* in place of the *t*. When Iooss took his marital vows, he did not say "I do." He said what New York Knicks announcer Marv Albert says when a Knick hits a shot: "Yesss!" Iooss and I once rode in a Chicago cab driven by Rosetta Shinboom.

Cabdrivers, as a class, have the most noteworthy names in America. There was one in the *New York Daily News* the other day named Just Ackah. And yet they are quite often quoted anonymously. This strikes me as fishy. The way I look at journalistic ethics, license to cite a cogent cabdriver should not be extended to anyone who cannot also make up a credible name: " 'Well,' observed U Gonxha, the Burmese-Albanian hackie who drove me in from the airport, 'what most folks around here are saying is . . .' "

Most folks are not cabdrivers. But when I was younger I could remember their names anyway. One weekend in Pittsburgh I must have introduced my wife to two hundred people, flawlessly except for a set of twins. (With twins I have always tried too hard. I get them down pat, and then I look at one or the other, and it's not as if I don't know which one it is, but I think, "Pat. Is this the one I am determined to remember is Pat, or isn't Pat?") That was ten years ago. Now names come to me like dreams: at first so vivid (*oh, I'll have no trouble holding on to this!*) and then gone.

I fault not only my age, which is advancing, but also the one we live in, which isn't. Names today are like dollars: there are far more of them than there used to be and they amount to less. Baseball players should all be mythical. But today there must be, among the Minnesota Twins alone, four or five semi-phenoms who have moved right on into budding sort-of-stardom without ever quite registering. There is a Teufel. If you held a knife to my throat, I couldn't tell you whether Teufel is pronounced as in "Teufel, Teufel / We adore thee" or to rhyme with "rueful." I just don't know. I don't know whether I ever will know.

But I can live with that. What bothers me is finding myself face-to-face with an actual human being who looks familiar, and who seems to know me (and why would he lie?), but whose name I am afraid I will not be able to dredge up until sometime next week, if then. Recently I spoke with my old college friend Lamar Alexander, who is now governor of Tennessee. (Which means that I can name one American governor. Didn't governors used to be more vivid?) I asked him how he managed to remember all the people he must shake hands with. His answer was, he didn't. He said that when somebody comes up to him with a certain sly grin and says, "I bet you don't remember my name," he often replies, "No, I bet I don't."

Why can't I do that? Why must I bluff and flounder? Why in the name of all that is holy do I say things like, "Oh! Hi! Great to see you again, ah, Hmblmbl"? What possesses me to plunge right into "Well! If it isn't . . ." at the same time that I am thinking, "What if, in fact, it's *not?*"?

It is time for me to face up to the fact that I can no longer place implicit trust in the tip of my tongue. I can no longer assume that I *virtually* remember the name in question and if I just forge ahead with an honest heart . . . After your mind reaches saturation, an honest heart can't carry it.

Not long ago I was autographing books in a city where I had worked some years before. No matter how bad your handwriting, you can't fake an inscription: "For Mmnlnnln — those were the days!" And if you say, "For the life of me, I can't remember the *spelling* . . ." then the answer will be:

"C-U-N . . ."

"Right, right . . ."

". . . N-I-N . . ."

"Oh, yeah, uh . . ."

". . . G . . . H . . ."

"Ohhh, sure, . . . uh . . ."

". . . A . . ."

"Oh! No! Of course! I don't mean the *Cunningham* part! I mean your *first* —"

"J-I-M."

So I was delighted to see none other than Old Greer Chastain (not his real name) in front of me. "Hey, Greer!" I sang out.

"This is old Greer Chastain," I informed the bookstore's proprietor. "Hell of a fisherman. Used to come into the office with a string that long of bass and bream and crappies and —"

"Shea Whislet," Greer said.

"What say, Greer?" I said.

"I'm Shea Whislet," he said. (Not his real name.)

"Oh," I said. "I . . . What's wrong with me! Thing is, I guess because you used to hang around so much with Greer Chastain, and —"

"Noo," he said, frowning.

"That's right! That's right! I don't know what made me . . . *Nobody* used to hang around with Greer Chastain! Nobody even *liked* Greer Chastain! He just stuck in my mind I guess because he was *so* unmemorable. Here, Shea, let me . . ."

Even though I made a point of not having to ask him how to spell "Shea," our grins were forced when he moved away and the next person came forward.

"I'm Greer Chastain," he said.

The other day I was playing tennis with my friend Lois Betts when a mutual acquaintance stopped by with his dog. I was almost entirely sure that this man was the one I thought he was, whose name I had heard many times, with whom I had chatted several times, and to whom I had often said, "Hi, how you doing?" I felt that if I strained for about five minutes I would know his name from Adam.

Furthermore, I felt that I would be able to stall for five minutes by focusing on the dog, whom I heard Lois call Bob. Unfortunately I am unable to focus *casually* on something I am not actually focusing on in my mind.

"Bob? Hey, that's a good name for a big old orange dog," I said, tousling Bob's ears. "What caused you to name him Bob?"

"No . . . it's Hobbit, actually," said the man.

"Oh," I said heartily. "Thought Lois said Bob. Well, you're a fine dog, Hobbit. Yes sir. Never knew a dog named Hobbit."

Meanwhile, I was thinking: *Don't babble. Concentrate. Wait a minute, it's coming. Is it . . . ? No, no, it probably isn't. Don't blurt it out! It probably isn't!*

"I had a dog named Bob when I was a kid," I went on. "Because of his tail. And then too, I had read *Bob, Son of Battle*. You know, that book by . . . Oh, you know. What's his name? I *know* his name, it's . . ."

Meanwhile, I was thinking: *Drop it. You've got enough to worry about.* This *man's name. Concentrate.*

"Old Bob, yep. I guess whenever I think of dogs, Bob's name comes to mind. He was my favorite dog."

Meanwhile, I was thinking: *He was not! You're lying about who your favorite dog was! Bob was no-account! Used to get lost all the time! Chipper was your favorite dog, and you know it! Somewhere in dog heaven, Bob is probably saying, "Hey, he never seemed to think I was all that great a dog when I was alive. Truth is I wasn't all that great a dog. I was always getting lost. He knows that. I never realized he was so shallow."*

After perhaps four and a half minutes, Hobbit and the man trotted off. I gazed after them, relieved and yet vexed. "Lois," I said, "What is —"

"Now *that*," said Lois, "was *awful*."

"Well," I said, "I was trying —"

"The *guy*'s name is Bob," she said.

I could, I guess, call all men "Colonel" or "Big Fella." That doesn't address the problem of what to call women. "Sister"? I don't think it would go over.

For that matter you have to be a certain kind of person to carry off calling people Colonel or Big Fella. You have to be a person on the order of Babe Ruth, who never made any pretense of remembering anyone's name, even longtime teammates'. Ruth called everyone "Jidge," a sort of affectionym for George, which was Ruth's real first name. I believe Bobo Newsom, the old pitcher, called everyone "Bobo." Or maybe it was Bobo Olson, the old fighter. I don't think I want to call everyone "Roy."

I am reminded, however, that Byron Saam, the Philadelphia Phillies' announcer, is said to have opened his broadcast once by exclaiming, "*Hello,* Byron Saam! This is everybody!"

If only one were, in fact, everyone else. Then the burden would be on them.

Simple Answers

Why Did the President Hit
Angie Dickinson?

Y OU know Ronald Reagan was originally set to play Rick in *Casablanca*. How different might the world be today if he'd done that, and Bogart had been elected President.

Bogie and Bacall in the White House! That would be something, wouldn't it? Old Gorbachev may be slick, but slicker than Sydney Greenstreet? I doubt it. You know what might have worked? The Carter administration with Bogart in the lead. Bogie wouldn't have had to force the toughness, and therefore could have done something with the sentimentality, the outsiderism, the crisis of confidence.

Bogart is all wrong for the Reagan years, of course, but who isn't? Caspar Weinberger resembles the late William Holden with a headache, and Suzanne Pleshette, if she took amiability suppressants, could pass for Ann Gorsuch Burford. George Kennedy, with his head hunched down into his shoulders, could be George Schultz. But I don't see much of a movie there. The President is too old to play himself, and no other actor projects his particular dispiriting innocence. Remember Gale Storm, of the old "My Little Margie" show? Perhaps she came closest.

As for Mrs. Reagan, well, let's see. Anybody want to speculate as to what it would be like if Jane Wyman were First Lady and Nancy were in "Falcon Crest"?

I didn't think so. The fascinating thing is that there is never anything interesting to say about the Reagans. Working oneself into a lather over them is like working oneself into a lather over, say, Mickey Rooney. It's not going to do any good. Just as there are always going to be a certain number of welfare cheats, there are always going to be a certain number of people like the Reagans. It has never been my feeling that such people should be at our nation's helm, but what do I know? I'm from Georgia.

In Laurence Leamer's revealing yet less than riveting book, *Make-Believe: The Story of Nancy and Ronald Reagan,* each Reagan gets typed pretty well. According to Clare Boothe Luce, Ron switched from left wing to right because "he was a healthy, normal guy who liked to saw wood. Then he started to socialize with the better class in L.A. People haven't liked to admit that the rich are often smarter and better."

It was Jefferson, I believe, who said that as cream rises naturally to the top, so too will the better class in L.A. Which is exactly Nancy's crowd. "Miss Donahue, Nancy's favorite saleslady at I. Magnin's, said of [Nancy and her friends], 'They're professional ladies,' referring to the profession of being a lady," Leamer says.

Leamer also discloses that, around Thanksgiving of 1960, Ron and Nancy played together in a "GE Theater" TV production of "A Turkey for the President."

The best observation about Ronnie in this book is Nancy's: "He doesn't understand undercurrents." He may not even have any. When he cried out, "Where's the rest of me?" in *King's Row* it may have been his undercurrents he was missing, not his legs.

Leamer does not indulge in any such speculation. Astonishingly, he doesn't even mention Reagan's last movie, *The Killers.* He does dig up a 1950 quote from Ron in *Silver Screen:*

"I'd love to be a louse. You know the kind of fellow who

leers at the dolls and gets leered back at? The guy who treats women rough and makes them love it . . . ? You know why I'd love to be a louse? Because the public loves him. He makes money for his employers. . . . And because the louse business is the sure, the open road to Fame in Films."

In *The Killers,* Ronald Reagan plays a louse. It is a strange feeling to watch the leader of the Free World aim a rifle down into the street from an overhead window (the movie was released within months after JFK's assassination) and shoot Clu Gulager and Lee Marvin. It is even stranger to watch him take a punch at Angie Dickinson and knock her flat.

Reagan is credible as a louse but not appealing, because he doesn't seem to take much relish in anything, even Angie. I don't know why commentators have focused so much on *Bedtime for Bonzo* and *Knute Rockne, All American,* when such a film as *The Killers* cries out for cinemo-political exegesis.

I do know why Reagan (who is so sweet to Nancy) hits Angie Dickinson, and also why Americans elected Reagan President. Tired of undercurrents.

Does Your Democrat Bite?

GARY HART won in New Hampshire. I was in Minnesota, Walter Mondale's state. The *St. Paul Sunday Pioneer Press* had a story: Hart knew how to talk on TV, Mondale didn't. Said an unnamed producer of network news:

"Hart speaks in sound bites: the fifteen- to twenty-second pithy statements that we absolutely must have to make a piece, statements with a beginning, a middle, and an end.

"When you try to cut into [Mondale], you always find that the complete thought he's developing has a lot of pieces and structures. He doesn't wrap it up well.

"It bothers me that you can't get the smartest people on TV just because they speak in dependent clauses."

The producer had used six dependent clauses himself. But he wasn't on TV, he just produced it. Maybe I was into too many pieces and structures myself. Maybe America was. I did some research. These are dependent clauses:

- ". . . that all men are created equal, that they are endowed by their Creator with certain inalienable Rights . . ."
- ". . . that in the field of public education the doctrine of 'separate but equal' has no place."
- ". . . whether that nation, or any nation so conceived and so dedicated, can long endure."

Fine. But America needs new initiatives. Fresh energy.

High concept. America responds to a person who will wrap it up. These are sound bites:

- "Give me liberty or give me death!"
- "Go for it!"
- "Damn the torpedoes! Full speed ahead!"

Sound bites turn people on. Do people dance to dependent clauses? "When the deep purple falls . . ." Not anymore. Now it's "Beat it, beat it, beat it!" and "Ma-ni-ac, ma-ni-ac!" I resolved to move toward sound bites myself.

Then Mondale won in Illinois.

I was confused. Confusion and sound bites don't mix. Time for more research. I went to a dinner party and found a network anchorman there.

Dinner-party statements by anyone above cabinet rank are not for attribution. So the anchorman will go nameless. I asked him about the anonymous producer's remarks. The anchorman spoke in a tone of professional appreciation:

"Right. I've just been cutting Hart. Everything he says is clip-clipty-clop, clip-clipty-clop."

The anchorman moved his hand in a crisp, vigorous way.

I had to like that rhythm. I spoke to our hostess. "Great baked ham." I took a good, sound bite. I was getting pithier and pithier.

Then Mondale won in New York.

"Maybe I'll ease partway back into dependent clauses," I said to myself. But it might be too late. I couldn't remember any subordinating conjunctions. I swallowed hard.

More research. I watched Shirley MacLaine on "60 Minutes." She was telegenic. She expressed firm opinions:

- You can learn from winning, you can learn from losing.
- There are no great people in politics anymore.
- The most brilliant poem ever written is Rudyard Kipling's "If."

Shirley MacLaine won the Academy Award.

I looked that poem up. It is almost all dependent clauses.

Then Mondale won in Pennsylvania.

My mouth was dry. I had gone for sound bites hook, line,

and sinker. Should I have kept at least one tooth in dependent clauses? I couldn't answer that question. Not in sound bites.

I needed more research.

I read a Mondale statement on winning in Pennsylvania: "This is a big win. . . . I would anticipate several tough fights down the road."

Ahhhh.

Relief at last.

Of course Mondale was winning! He had caught on to sound bites. Probably read about them in the *Sunday Pioneer Press.* I thought back. When had Mondale brought his campaign into focus? After New Hampshire. How? By saying, "Where's the beef?"

I read a Hart statement on losing in Pennsylvania: "If it gets down to a candidate running for President, in effect, on the backs of only one constituent group, I think that doesn't say much for the ability of the candidate to broaden that base."

Hart had drifted into dependent clauses.

Not me. Clipty-clop. I wouldn't say "if" if I had a mouthful of it.

Shirley MacLaine may be right. But not about that poem.

On Point of View

It's not just a question of what they say,
But also of who is "they."
When cannibals speak of a gourmet dinner,
They mean that they ate a gourmet.

Do Camp and Lit Mix?
(A Letter Home)

Dear Unnatural Parent,

IT is 7:12 P.M. Dusk drags sunswollen feet. In the distance, strings are played (tennis: *fwok, fwok*). Through the wall, I hear adenoidal voices arguing the feasibility of an unpublished poets' union. Some squat, indifferently plumed bird is gawping, insentiently, into my window. I am at literary camp. Hurrah.

I *could* be at home, snug in my own room, munching fresh Mallomars and putting one more polish on Canto Five ("Greed Disgorges the Knight of Love"), but no. *You* insisted I come to Paper Mountain Writers' Conference. Do you know, Next of Kin, what we do every morning? Every morning we do deconstruction. I *defy* deconstruction, anytime, anywhere. We are invited to deconstruct at 6:15 A.M., *outdoors.* Forty-five minutes' supposed disabuse of our own texts, *sur l'herbe.* It is designed to tone us up.

Pah!

"Young people my own age" you desired me to meet. My roommate is a forty-seven-year-old driver of an Avis airport shuttle bus who is writing an account of his travels. Since 1972 he has been negotiating one 3.8-mile circle thirty to thirty-five times daily. "For eleven solid years," he told me, "I tell myself, 'Leland, this ain't no career. This ain't *leading* anywhere, Leland.' But then I took this writing course at the junior college, and the prof said, 'Leland, write what you know.' "

To begin with, he wrote rondels.

Rondels!

"Rondels are dead!" I told him. "Small things are dead! Verse is dead! Nothing *can* live save the major protean. We must return in one enormous motion to the epic-poetic and the great prose models!"

"Yeah," he said. "I tell myself, 'Leland, if you put together a long enough *sequence* of rondels . . .' But then I figure, 'Leland, old buddy, let's get practical: no movie in it. So let's do it first as a novelized version. Take the money. Run. Then we've bought ourselves some time.' "

Leland!

"Influential people in the writing business" you desired me to meet. Last night there was a cocktail party in the Founder's Residence. One popular (except among all those people who have met him) biographer of robber barons and dubious empresses exchanging insider-talk with a peer:

"How many cities on your promotional tour?"

"Ten."

"Really? I did seventeen cities myself."

"Yes, but mine weren't all in the same state."

One novelist I have vaguely heard of (but whose novels I would not touch with a fifty-foot drop line) to another and vice versa:

"You know, my last book sold quite well."

"Like hotcakes, I understand. But, then, the reviews were so flat."

"They were not. They were *mixed.*"

"Oh, that's right — I understand you shredded them all yourself."

Do I need this? I do not. Is this sublime? It is not. Does

this stir up something new from ancient depths; does this bid fair to ricochet from age to age to age? Yes, and Kleenex is the Golden Fleece.

None of the so-called established writers at this chickadee-infested retreat seem to have read anyone except whoever of their number has just left the room, which gives those remaining an opportunity to remark that the departed one has evinced, in his latest overpraised offering, a failure of nerve.

As you know, I refuse to show my manuscript to anyone who is incapable of reading something larger than himself. Accordingly, I have not shown it to anyone here. Today I had a "conference" with my "adviser," none other than Edward Noone, the author of *Hurled.* "Do you have anything to show me?" he asked.

"We'll see," I said.

That seemed to throw him. A silent moment passed. "So, uh, who do you read — who're you influenced by?" he inquired, assuming no doubt that the first words out of my mouth would be "Well, aside from *you,* of course . . ."

"Scott," I said.

He brightened. "Oh, you know Scott Spencer?"

"Sir Walter," I snapped.

He looked startled.

"And, now that you mention it, Edmund."

No, not startled. He looked *afraid.* As if he had asked whether I had any pets, and I had handed him Bucephalus, Leviathan, a breathing Sphinx. *Grandeur* is not a notion to these people. They shrink — which had seemed impossible — at the merest whiff of esemplastic sweep.

Another silent moment. "I believe," I said, "that *you* have nothing to show *me.*" And then I left him with his word processor, which I hear he gnaws.

"Nice young women who share my interests" you desired me to meet. The only female I have seen here who is not hoping, by all appearances, that her tube-top will snag her some pull with a prizewinning poetaster or at least with a tall editor of a small magazine is one Ariel Garms — who yesterday, with one swing of her still inchoate yet rather pursy autobiography, squashed the septum of an already nasal specialist in acquisitional lunching who was offering her counsel on publishers' advances. She claimed he made one. Perhaps you think me bashful to a fault. Yet and still (to employ the favorite locution of Reid Whiteblood, the tenured South Carolinian ironist who chairs our daily neo-ambiguity sessions), I steer clear.

Also in attendance here: a married couple who have been driving around the nation eating chocolate chip cookies *du pays,* taking copious notes, and working up a guidebook they plan to turn into a musical about a couple falling in love while searching America for the perfect cookie. (Their working title: "Looky!") They seek pointers, never having taken on anything of this magnitude before.

Chocolate chip cookies!

To think that I am wasting my substance in a place where I must acknowledge, even to myself, that there exist people into whose minds even an inkling of such a subliterate project could filter!

Ah. Ah. I hear your puncturing voice. Yes. Yes. In the absence of Mallomars, I *do eat* chocolate chip cookies, for creative energy. And so would have Victor Hugo, had there been chocolate chip cookies in his time. But I *would not write about* chocolate chip cookies. Any more than I would write about the several distinct rashes I have acquired during my idyll on this green mountain, from various poisonous plants and an institutional alfresco diet. The people here would, though. I do not doubt for one instant that people here are at this very moment pounding out leadenly minimalistic short-story collections based on remarks and glances passed during the "buzz session" following this afternoon's advisory on garnering invitations to conduct workshops on "Writing the Work in Progress" when a *proposal* for a work in progress is all that one has yet produced.

Fwok. Fwok. A tennis *tournament* is slated for this weekend. Top-seeded is a former investigative reporter from Sacramento who is said to be nearly finished with a rush-job novel about a President and a Vice-President who are having an affair that Muammar el-Qaddafi cottons onto. A sure guide: the trashier an author's themes, the more heavily muscled his right forearm.

A lecture is scheduled for tomorrow evening. "How to Break Through." By an émigré Australian, so possessed of divine afflatus that (according to a notice stapled to a tree that leans dangerously over the path to the lecture hall and is swarming with ants) he "reviews for many periodicals." His name is Osip. I believe assumed.

Tomorrow there will be a picnic on the raft in the middle of Lake Sotweed. One is expected, it would appear, to paddle out there on one's own steam, in one's trunks. Did Milton swim?

Pfaugh!

This afternoon I was called "unprofessional" by an aspiring children's playwright.

So you have had your desire. A Paper Mountain camper am I, hey nonny nonny. Today I saw an immense snake. "Ah," I apostrophized the serpent, from a hastily quadrupled distance, "you must know my mother, Eve. Give her my best, when you see her next over some new woe-fraught apple she has in mind forcing between the teeth of her only son, whose narrative gift he must somehow shield and nurture all on his own against cheeseheads, pharisees, and probably-anopheles mosquitoes because she thinks it is good for him."

Now I go to hear an agent read.

> *Your abandoned issue,*
> *Gavin*

Who's the Funniest American Writer?

M ARK TWAIN.
Who's the most essential?
Same answer.
What other nation can make that claim?
Now: What are the three great American things?
Jazz, the Bill of Rights, and Mark Twain.
Where did they all come from?
The South.
That's right. Jazz came together in New Orleans; the Bill
of Rights came from the Virginia Declaration of Rights; and
Samuel Clemens was conceived in Tennessee of Kentucky
parents, was born in Missouri and reared there among slaves
and hardscrabble whites on the banks of the Mississippi
River, and got his pen name from his days as a pilot on that
river. He fought, ingloriously, for the Confederacy, which
would have been a lot better off had it followed his example
and demilitarized after two weeks.

But Mark Twain scarcely set foot in Dixie for the last
two-thirds of his life. (Jazz also moved up the river, and the
Bill of Rights has never been entirely at home in the South.)
In his prime as author and paterfamilias he resided at 351
Farmington Avenue in Hartford, Connecticut. Sixty thou-

sand pilgrims visit his house every year. In its parking lot recently sat a Cadillac from Florida whose bumper sticker read:

GOD SAID IT
I BELIEVE IT
THAT SETTLES IT

Mark Twain didn't settle that easily. You don't know about Mark Twain without you have read a book by the name of *Mr. Clemens and Mark Twain,* by Justin Kaplan, of Cambridge, Mass. According to that book neither of them, Clemens or Twain, knew whether he was coming or going half the time.

Let's say Jehovah had dropped into Hartford, suddenly filled Mark Twain's billiard room one afternoon and said:

sam, What you Ought To Do Is Get On Back Down South, Amidst All That Backwoods And Afro-American Hellaciousness And Juice That Is your True Soul. Maybe Build you A Big Place In Memphis And Invent Rock and Roll Early.

I doubt Mark Twain would have heeded. By the time he moved to Hartford, he was too much into big commerce, New England respectability, and machinery. William Dean Howells, the Boston literary Brahmin out of Columbus, Ohio, said Mark Twain "was the most desouthernized Southerner I ever knew."

And Mark Twain didn't trust God. Any further than he could throw Him. Another thing you ought to read before you visit Mark Twain's house is a poem by Robert Penn Warren (who himself has migrated from Kentucky to Vermont). This poem, "Last Laugh," tells how eleven-year-old Sam Clemens watched through a keyhole as his father, always distant, was cut open and partly dissected by way of postmortem. (Incidentally, when Richard Pryor, the funniest living American, was a boy he watched through a keyhole as his mother turned tricks.) And how Sam went on to become almost hysterically, though straight-facedly, funny, professionally. And how he chaffed his beloved wife, Livy, out of her faith, then saw her die without its consolations, "And was left alone with his joke, God dead, till he died."

But what you mostly ought to read is *The Adventures of Huckleberry Finn,* which Ernest Hemingway said was the beginning of American fiction, and several hundred thousand other words of Mark Twain's stuff, which is dark inside but makes you smile profoundly.

The same may be said of his High Victorian Gothic dream house. Nineteen mostly crepuscular but spirited rooms, kaleidoscopically decorated by Louis Tiffany. And a ground-floor gallery where I viewed, among other mementos, a slate on which Twain would jot notes to himself. The slate, I am pleased to report, was not left clean. Few of the overlapping scribbles are decipherable, but I did make out two sensible reminders:

> *Leave the cat here.*
> *Take the whiskey along.*

Insofar as Clemens/Twain ever settled, he did it in this house — from 1874, when it was built at his behest, to 1891, when business fiascoes compelled him to close it and go lecturing and writing abroad for big money. During these seventeen years he wrote most of his best books, including *The Adventures of Huckleberry Finn, The Adventures of Tom Sawyer,* and *Life on the Mississippi,* and he enjoyed his (doomed) family life to its fullest.

I envy him his billiard room, where Mark Twain repaired to drink, smoke cigars, and curse. He also wrote in that room, but not much, because he shot a lot of billiards, entertained a plenitude of literati and Union generals, and pursued bad business deals.

It is clear why the house suited him: it's a house with a lot of nerve, its exterior made of red, black, and vermilion brick, with deep-red wood trim and a jauntily gabled, tricolor, diamond-patterned roof. But Hartford? This is a question that interests me particularly, as I am myself a writer from the South who has wound up in New England, an area that I find — generally speaking — more tasteful than Georgia but less tasty. At least I live in the woods of New England. Hartford?

Well, you may write like an angel in the South, but unless you can get those northern publishing gears to turn for you, you are not an American writer. Hartford was a big publishing city in Mark Twain's day, and less stuffy than Boston, the capital of American lit — handy enough to Boston, however, that Twain could develop a close friendship with Howells, who reviewed him glowingly and published him prestigiously in the *Atlantic*, which, as Twain put it, "don't require a 'humorist' to paint himself stripèd and stand on his head every fifteen minutes."

For reasons of both the wallet and the spirit, Mark Twain always wanted to write for as many people as possible. (Toward the end of his life, in fact, he set aside an antilynching book so as not to alienate his southern readers.) He first visited Hartford in 1868 to meet the publisher of his first full-scale book, *The Innocents Abroad,* which made him rich and famous. He saw elegant lawns and, for the first time, huckleberries. "I never saw any place," he wrote, "where morality and huckleberries flourished as they do here."

Hartford also boasted a well-to-do literary community called Nook Farm, where Mark Twain's mansion was erected a stone's throw from that of the author of *Uncle Tom's Cabin.* Later on Harriet Beecher Stowe became a neighbor most notable for vigorous senility, which moved her, as Twain put it, to "slip up behind a person who was deep in dreams and musings and fetch a war whoop that would jump that person out of his clothes." But she represented literary respectability and social prominence, partly because her brother was the eminent minister Henry Ward

Beecher, who, as a matter of fact, was tried in court for adultery with a parishioner the year after Twain's Hartford house was built (the case ended in a hung jury).

Had Twain encountered the Reverend Beecher's shame or Mrs. Stowe's whoops as a young man in the South or the West he would surely have relished them, worked them into yarns. But in Hartford, at early middle age, he found them unsettling. He had been roving, escaping various things, since his boyhood. Like Huck Finn he felt trapped by civilizing influences, but he also sought them out, because (also like Huck Finn to some extent) he felt a growing aversion to redneckery. "Ignorance, intolerance, egotism, self-assertion, opaque perception, dense and pitiful chuckleheadedness — and an almost pathetic unconsciousness of it all. That is what I was at nineteen and twenty; and that is what the average Southerner is at sixty today," he wrote in 1876.

But to get away from all that takes more than a geographical move. As Mark Twain aged in New England, his image of the people he sprang from became his image of people in general, not to mention himself. In 1882 he wrote Howells: "Oh, hell, there is no hope for a person who is built like me; — because there is no cure, no cure. If I could only *know* when I have committed a crime: then I could conceal it & not go stupidly dribbling it out, circumstance by circumstance, into the ears of a person who will give no sign till the confession is complete; & then the sudden damnation drops on a body like the released pile-driver, & he finds himself in the earth down to his chin. When he merely supposed he was being entertaining."

He was, of course, being entertaining. He was ripping and snorting, and not just joyfully. Wherever he lighted he could not get disentangled from his own lacerating fruitful complex of self-innocence and remorse. Much as he doted on them, his daughters — when he learned this he felt terrible guilt — were frightened by his bellowing. One genteel Hartford Sabbath morning he flung open his bathroom window and hurled shirts and sulphurous language from it, because of a button problem.

There were high times in Hartford, though. Once, the Thomas Bailey Aldriches and other proper literary Bostonians visited. They were met by Mark Twain's carriage, driven by a liveried coachman, with Mark Twain's butler riding footman. Dinner was luxurious. The next morning Mark Twain knocked on the Aldriches' door and stiffly accused them of disturbing the household with their bedroom noises. Only at the breakfast table did the mortified couple learn that their host was pulling their legs. In the evening after dinner he astonished the visiting gentry in another way by singing, in a pleasant but eerie voice, "Swing Low, Sweet Chariot" and "Go Down, Moses." Then, as Justin Kaplan describes it, he "changed from his evening slippers into something considerably odder for Hartford, white cowskin moccasins with the hair on the outside. And, in a crowning act of confident alienation from his guests, he twisted his body into the likeness of a crippled uncle or a Negro at a hoe-down and danced strange dances for them. Howells always remembered . . . the joy and disoriented surprise of the guests."

That must have made Mark Twain feel oriented for a while. But he craved a more lasting fix. Unfortunately for him, one of Hartford's industries was the Colt arms factory. That was where Hank Morgan, hero of *A Connecticut Yankee in King Arthur's Court,* worked; it was from the Colt plant that Morgan was transported to Camelot, where his mechanical know-how awed and eventually alienated ignorant, intolerant sixth-century England. Mark Twain, whose first profession had been manual typesetting, was Connecticut Yankee enough to love machines, but he loved them in what seems to me a southern way: as if they were flesh and blood and also metaphysical. He desired an anthropomorphic machine without human flaw.

At the Colt factory he saw an early working model of the

Paige typesetting machine. Into the development of this wondrous device Mark Twain plunged years of his time and almost two hundred thousand dollars of his and wife Livy's fortunes. "In two or three weeks," he wrote his brother, "we shall work the stiffness out of her joints and have her performing as smoothly and softly as human muscles." But the machine — which he estimated would earn him fifty-five million dollars a year — was always too high-strung to be practical. It resides now in the basement gallery of his house. Its failure was the main reason Mark Twain had to move.

His favorite daughter, Susy, stayed behind in Hartford — staying with friends but regularly visiting Mark Twain's now deserted house — as the rest of the family roamed. While they were gone she contracted meningitis, began going blind, took up some paper in Mark Twain's house (she showed writing promise herself), and scrawled deliriously: "Mr. Clemens, Mr. Zola, Mr. Harte, I see that even darkness can be great. To me darkness must remain from everlasting to everlasting." She died before the family could get back home. They were on their way to solvency by then, but they could never stand to live in the house again.

In 1903 it was sold to the Richard Bissell family.* It later housed a boys' school, then a library. Now it's a shrine. On my recent tour of the house, we were admonished not to touch anything, but I did sneak one turn of a doorknob. George Griffin, Mark Twain's butler, is described by Kaplan as a gambler and a moneylender to Hartford's black community. Our guide, Carolyn Volpe, said it was Griffin's duty, when there were guests for dinner, to sit behind a screen in the dining room, awaiting discreet commands from Livy; but he would betray his presence by beginning to laugh, ahead of the punch line, at Mark Twain's stories, which he had heard

*Richard Bissell, Jr., the CIA official who authored the Bay of Pigs fiasco, was born in Mark Twain's house. Richard P. Bissell, who wrote funny novels about the Mississippi (and in fact was the first author licensed as a pilot on that river since Mark Twain), was born in Dubuque. Go figure.

before. Livy would fire him for these lapses, and Mark Twain would hire him back.

Our guide pointed out the door to Griffin's room upstairs. It hadn't been restored, she said. "We don't know what it looked like, because he was the only one who went in there."

Didn't Marse Mark ever pop in? Maybe the two of them would get together in there and sing a spiritual, share a pipe, or even josh about how they ought to take a raft down the Mississippi as Huck and the slave Jim did — Huck having decided, against all the strictures of civilized religion as he knew it, to commit the great crime of Mark Twain's fiction: helping a sold man get free.

I wanted to know what it was like in there. I stuck my head in, heard a hum, saw metal ducts. Modern-day heating. A machine.

Salute to the Bear

Do you reckon Mark Twain and Paul "Bear" Bryant ever sit around in Heaven chewing the fat?

"What is Man?" muses Twain, who tends to get off into that kind of thing.

"Well," says the Bear, choosing to believe that the subject is pass defense, "there's Man and there's Zone. Down home I was always partial to Man, myself. Wasn't anything technical about it. Just one old knotty-headed boy trying to haul in a projectile and anothun trying to change his mind."

"I know of a bear," says Twain (having been brought back to firmer ground), "that crossed paths with a missionary. The question arose, who would convert whom? The matter stood unresolved for only a short time. Thereafter the bear held to his ursine ways, and the missionary walked in the paths of the bear — or all of him did, I mean to say, except his eternal soul and his India rubber boots."

"A bear don't mince words," says Bryant.

Bear Bryant's teams — most notably at the University of Alabama — won more games than any other coach's in college football history. While he lived, Alabamians told this story:

One day in Heaven a figure went stomping importantly by, wearing a whistle and a cap with an *A* on it, and a newcomer asked, "Who is that?" A longtime resident answered, "God — but he thinks he's Bear Bryant."

They also said Bryant was the only coach ever to have an animal named after him, but in fact he earned his nickname when he wrestled a traveling bear in a movie theater in Fordyce, Arkansas, where he grew up dirt poor. I have spent only ten or twelve days in Arkansas in my life, but I have already met two different people who claimed they witnessed that event. One of them said that he, in a suit, was the bear; but he was drinking and I believe he would have said anything. In Arkansas. I don't think he would have said that around many folks in Alabama.

Let me interject here that I was once surrounded in a Birmingham hotel lobby by a swarm of drunks in red hats and miracle-fiber suits who were saying "Roll Tide" to one another. ("Roll Tide" is what fans of the Alabama Crimson Tide say the way other people say "What it is?" or "Shalom.") And I didn't like it. On the whole I would rather be surrounded in an airport by those kids who try to sell you *Back to Godhead* magazine. That's how much I didn't like it. But I never quarreled with the notion that Bear Bryant looked like God. That's what quarterback George Blanda, an extremely craggy person himself, thought thirty-some-odd years ago when he saw Bryant's granite face for the first time. When I saw the Bear for the first time up close, briefly in 1972, he had the hardest eyes I'd ever seen. Deep, like Raymond Burr's, but a lot colder.

One of the things that persuaded Bryant to leave Texas A & M in 1957 and return to Alabama, his alma mater, was that he had been receiving bagfuls of letters from Alabama grammar-school kids who said they wanted to play for him if he ever came back. Was he perceived, then, as a kindly, understanding figure who would ease a boy's way through the hard knocks of big-time ball? Well, hell no, he wasn't. The Bear was known for his sign that read BE GOOD OR BE GONE. When he overheard players so much as hint that they had

had enough of his slave-driving drills, he "cleaned their lockers for them and piled their clothes out in the hall," as he recalls in *Bear,* his rousing 1974 memoir written with John Underwood. "I'd make them prove what they had in their veins, blood or spit, one way or the other." Bryant would take a bad team and push it so ferociously over rough and blistered ground that the kind of player he disliked, the player accustomed to getting by on natural gifts rather than on hunger, would quit. After the Bear's first spring practice at Texas A & M, only 27 players were left out of the 115 who originally reported. And people with a taste for soft living don't even *drive through* College Station, Texas, much less enroll in school there and go out for football. Bryant liked the player "who doesn't have any ability but doesn't know it." He liked country boys like himself — in his last years they tended to be black, he said — who would do anything to get away from the dusty, grinding, ungratifying labor in their backgrounds. The Bear would give them even heavier dust, harder grinding, and less sweetness than they were used to. He would get down in the dirt with them and fight. He would hardly ever give them a kind word. He would rasp the bunch of them down to a hard core that could beat all comers at "eleven man and sic 'em" football and then graduate with a will into pro ball, coaching, or business. (How would you like a man like Bear Bryant to come over to your house to sell you insurance? "You ain't got enough coverage and you know it! Just git on out of this house and turn this nice woman and these pretty babies out in the street if you ain't man enough to insure 'em. Go on! Go on! If you don't hurry I'm gonna set fire to your car!")

But what place did a man like that have in a university? Especially since the Bear in his own scholar-athlete days seldom went to class. He barely earned a phys ed degree from Alabama back when such degrees came even less hard than they do today.

Look at it this way, though: what if courses in education

were taught in the kind of language and at the kind of pitch in which and at which the Bear taught football? I'll tell you what: the nation's educators would make more sense.

They wouldn't be saying, "Evaluative procedures for the implementation of program goals and objectives have been identified, formulated, and prioritized based on acceptable criteria in order to foster enhanced positive learning experientialization."

They would be saying, "What you got to do is, keep your weight low to the ground, get your head in under the student's rib cage, and thrust upward. And *drive*. And by God if he don't learn what you're trying to teach him then, he must know something you don't. Or else not know something you thought he did. And you got to find out which it is and what it is — what*ever* it is — and come right back at him."

(I have tried and tried and tried to write the above passage in gender-unspecific terms. It won't work. We need a new pronoun. For one thing.)

I'm not trying to tell you that a college-football education resonates with human values. One evening in the early 1970s, a distinguished Tide lineman went before an audience of freshman players with a live squirrel he had just captured bare-handed on campus. He proceeded to rip the struggling animal apart, exclaiming as the blood flew, "This is what you got to do to win!" and then chewed on one of the torn-off legs. Poets, scientists, and department heads do comparably destructive things, though, and college teaching might make more sense and a deeper impression if it were more sanguineous. You always wonder what you might have learned if you'd had the chance to be scourged for a while by somebody who, like a standing dire emergency, was dreadfully good at getting some version of the most out of people.

The University of Alabama is not the nation's most rigorous academic institution. They say it is almost impossible to get anybody to take a class there after 2:00 P.M. But a hundred football players — some of them good students and all of them under pressure to absorb something one way or another — don't drag down a student body of 17,300. On the other hand, what might be the effect on a university if it had a *learning* team? Spurring one another on. Reaching down deep. Stressing fundamentals.*

In 1977 I went down to Tuscaloosa to confront the Bear. I entered his office at nine-thirty one morning. He was a big, fleshy sixty-four-year-old man, sprawled and restive behind his big sleek desk. The walls were paneled like a corporation exec's, except for the built-in blackboards. On one of these, different hands had chalked "26/47 Belly" and "I love you, Grandpoppa. Love, S.G.B."

I told the Bear that people were wondering whether college was worth it anymore. What did he, as a man who had done a lot of teaching that helped bring people out of poverty, think of that? How would he motivate students today?

He shrugged, not just modestly, and said he didn't know.

"Wouldn't it be interesting if other subjects were taught the way you've taught football?"

Maybe you have heard Kris Kristofferson on one of his albums introduce his song "To Beat the Devil" in a grave just-post-deep-deep-hangover talking bass: "I came across a great and wasted friend of mine . . . I saw he was about one step away from dying, and I couldn't help but wonder why." The Bear's voice sounded like that, but he was saying, "I certainly don't think football is as important as English or some academic department. Except that it's hard to get a crowd out to watch an examination."

His eyes were a lot less imposing than I remembered. He hadn't gotten to work until nine. He used to get in every morning at five-thirty, after stopping off somewhere on the way to throw up from the tension. In the old days he had

---

*In 1972, Kent Hannon, then of *Sports Illustrated*, interviewed Coach Bryant in his office and noticed on the bookshelf a copy of *Portnoy's Complaint*. Asked whether he had been reading such a book, the Bear denied any knowledge of what it contained or how it got there. I have never known what to make of this. Did he use it in preparing hygiene lectures for his boys?

spent evenings confronting his players in their dorm rooms. Now he hung out a lot at night at the Indian Hills Country Club.

"I wish to heck I'd gotten an education. I think it'd be more fun. If I could go speak to the Rotary Club and not use the same old adjectives over and over . . ."

I told him I'd never heard anybody complain about his adjectives.

"I'd study grammar. When I follow Bud Wilkinson at a coaching clinic, it's like daylight and dark, and I'm the dark."

That the Bear could think himself less eloquent than old network-bland Bud Wilkinson astounded me. In his book Bryant tells how he presented himself for the first time to a thousand Texas Aggies:

"I took off my coat and stomped on it.

"Then I took off my tie and stomped on it.

"Then, as I was walking up to the mike, I rolled up my sleeves."

Here, in his office, he already had his coat and tie off.

"I don't know," he said. "I don't know whether you ever motivate 'em or not. I doubt I have. . . . My old players get together now and talk about things that happened; I don't even remember. Got to look ahead to the next day. . . . Up until a few years ago I didn't do anything but work. Now other people are doing the work, most of it anyway. I'm trying to learn to relax. I don't read many books. Watch television — John Wayne, Bob Hope."

I asked him, "If you were to go back and take a course that you missed out on, what would it be?"

"I'd go back and take spelling."

Well, people had been telling me that the Bear had mellowed a lot. Investments had made him rich. In his book he had said he didn't try to "bleed and gut" players anymore; he tried to save them. He was letting them grow their hair longish. Communication was the key today, he said. He couldn't get down and scuffle with them anymore.

Maybe now God and the Bear sit around mellowing together. With John Wayne. I bet it galls all three of them, though, that the Duke, who had been the Bear's choice to portray him in his autobiographical movie, didn't live long enough.

To tell the truth, I thought that at some point during my visit with him the Bear would say something that would make me jump, like "Boy! Run through that brick wall over there and write a sharp account of whatever scene is on the other side. And I don't want to pick up one damn iota of overt reference to the wall." And I would have seriously considered doing it.

What he did say was, "You come back and see us now."

As I left the field house, a voice in my mind started spluttering, "*What?* That ain't the way to do a damn interview. That is a mean man back there. He has been known to hang out with Frank Sinatra and Spiro Agnew. You going to let him get away with all that crap about wishing he knew grammar and about English being more important than football?"

"Yeah," I told the voice. "I am. I think he's right."

What's So Humorous?

"OF the three types of convulsion," according to some notes I took years ago from a report on a conference on Cybernetics and Humor, "laughter is the one for which there is the clearest ideational content."

Aren't there more types of convulsion than that? Sneeze, Paroxysm, Orgasm, Upchuck, and Heart Attack spring to mind. If I were writing an allegory in which the Bland Knight manages to pass through the Vale of Convulsion with his guide, the sorely pressed Equanimity, those would all be characters. I can see Sneeze and Upchuck now. And how about Hiccup?

Another note from that cybernetics report: "There are two types of tickling." Left-handed and right-handed? Sweet and mean? Literal and figurative? Ribs and feet? All we may say for certain is, it is hard to discuss Humor without seeming a fool.

Hence, books of Humor receive little serious critical attention. There may well be thousands of close readers who would agree with me that Bruce Jay Friedman's *Lonely Guy's Book of Life,* for example, is a much better book, line for line and in toto, than many a bloated, enervating major comic novel such as John Barth's *Giles Goat-Boy* or John Irving's

World According to Garp. But no one ever says so in print.

However, if there is anything less dignified than setting up as a humorist, it is setting up as a humorist who is not taken seriously enough. A funny writer probably ought just to be laughed at, at least until old age, when he or she deserves to be genuinely nasty and revered.

Mordecai Richler, a truly funny writer but one who has had the wisdom to become a serious novelist, has collected *The Best of Modern Humor.* His sole criterion for the material he chose, he says in his introduction, was that "it had to make me laugh." That is hard to argue with. But somebody's got to do it.

First, however, I will declare my interest. I am one of the sixty-four writers anthologized, and I am also mentioned favorably in the introduction (to avoid any conflict, please skip over that passage, which is on page xvii, toward the bottom). As a lad, I read anthologies and figured that, if I could myself reach the point of being anthologized, I would be set. In my near-maturity I find that an anthologee's lot is not glorious. He is liable, browsing in a bookstore all innocently, to stumble upon himself in *Trees: A Golden Treasury of the Best Arboreal Writing of the Ages.* Never is there a prepublication card in the mail proclaiming, "Congratulations! You are hereby one of the great tree writers of all time." Since *The Best of Modern Humor* reached the stores, I have spoken to four of the writers appearing in it. Two of them were unaware that there was such a book. I gather that all I am ever going to see out of the deal, financially, is $67.50.

When my high-school classmates were tearing apart '51 Fords and inserting new cams and mufflers, I was getting just as greasy reading *A Subtreasury of American Humor,* edited by E. B. and Katherine S. White. That book appeared in 1941, the year of my birth. This new collection is the most definitive-looking roundup of literary American humor since, and it also embraces various top-notch Brits and V. S. Naipaul. Here are heroes of my adolescence — Robert Benchley, James Thurber, S. J. Perelman, H. L. Mencken, E. B. White, A. J. Liebling, Ring Lardner, and so on. Here too are at least seven contemporaries of mine with whom I have had too much to drink. I always wanted to be on a mythical all-star team.

And now that I am on one — these should have been Neil Armstrong's first words on the moon — it is not exactly what I had in mind. This book has a great deal of wonderful stuff in it, including Mencken on cops, Liebling on Earl Long, John Mortimer on schooldays, Eudora Welty on family life, Thomas Meehan on introducing Yma to Oona, Veronica Geng's "My Mao," Woody Allen on one man's Emma Bovary, and J. B. Morton's grandly ineffable "Intrusions of Captain Foulenough."

But Flann O'Brien, who may have been the funniest writer ever, is inadequately represented by some of his Keats and Chapman gags, one of which I don't get. I'd rather have had something from Peter De Vries and Kenneth Tynan other than their respective Faulkner parodies. (Trying to send up Faulkner is like trying to do an impression of Little Richard. You had better be able to cut loose.) Richler's Thurber selection is a pale one. And I have never cared much for Frank Sullivan's "Cliché Expert" pieces. I prefer the Whites' choice from Sullivan, "Gloria Swanson Defends Her Title," which has a magnetic hat in it; I am a sucker for anything with a magnetic hat.

At the time of the Whites' anthology, it was pretty clear what Humor was in this country. It was funny writing that had come out in the *New Yorker* or that people assumed had come out in the *New Yorker*. Parodies, sketches, personal essays, short stories, reporting, verse. For the prose, the *New Yorker* had and still has an infelicitous but suggestive term, "the casual." Implied is a straight-faced, graceful, deftly self-conscious flouting of rigidities and . . . oh God, I've got to get out of this kind of thing. There are two types of exit from this kind of thing, and that is one of them.

The other is to invoke the White House. We are seeing a resurgence of Humor in this country, as in the Harding and Coolidge administrations. My theory is that Humor flourishes in times of chipper but ill-advised composure.

In high school I decided that writing Humor was my vocation. I assumed there would be a good living in it. When I got out of college in 1963, however, there was not. This was partly because I was not as good at Humor as I had been in high school and partly because of the historical moment. Humor is counterrevolutionary. So are the great majority of revolutions, within a few months, but that was not a point that seemed called for in the sixties. In the sixties we had the Theater of the Absurd and Black Humor, neither of which was funny.

J. D. Salinger and Donald Barthelme had borne the *New Yorker* tradition of Humor off into, respectively, mysticism (or New Hampshire) and experimental fiction. Humor collections were scarce, pale, and ill-selling. Magazines kept saying they were always on the lookout for good Humor pieces, but rarely did they, the *New Yorker* included, find any.

Big shifts had to occur. I recall the lurid — no, the wholesome — exhilaration I felt on seeing the advance excerpt from *Portnoy's Complaint* in *Partisan Review*. Philip Roth had done what Zooey couldn't. He had brought explicit sex into Humor. It was about time. Humor as represented by the *Subtreasury* had always bordered on the prudish — had indeed (see Thurber) derived much of its energy from sexuality abashed and redirected. That did not work anymore.

Another thing that struck me as pivotal was the deep structural drollery of Norman Mailer's referring to himself as "Mailer" and as a "radical conservative" in *Armies of the Night*. Mailer the Committed was not right-thinking but loopy, recombinant and foxy. But although Mailer, like Kafka, has complained that readers miss his jokes, Humor was not his line. And Roth was not writing Humor pieces.

I did not begin to feel that Humor piecework was coming back as an occupational possibility until Nora Ephron's *Esquire* columns on women were collected as *Crazy Salad,* a best-seller. In one of those columns Ephron said she had grown up wanting to be Dorothy Parker and to write for the *New Yorker,* but she had gotten over both those ambitions. In the process, however, she had resolved matters of modern womanhood on the level of Humor. This was no small step for mankind.

Then, in *Rolling Stone,* Hunter S. Thompson took drugs out of the realm of stuporous religiosity and into Humor of a hellacious, wolverine-ridden kind. Along the way, at some cost to his cogency, he did American culture the service of running controlled substances into the ground.

Meanwhile Humor reached out in many directions. Woody Allen brought in Freud; Wilfrid Sheed actually wrote funny literary criticism; Fran Lebowitz put starch into Camp; Garrison Keillor blended the spirits of E. B. White and Saint Francis of Assisi; Calvin Trillin found merriment in food, demography, and leftism.

The Best of Modern Humor reflects this opening up and renewal of the old *Subtreasury* tradition. All the writers I have mentioned, except for Mailer and (regrettably) Hunter Thompson, are represented. The aforementioned *Portnoy* excerpt is included; and Ephron's robust piece on being flat-chested; and Trillin's savory column on the de la Rentas' salon, in which he refers to himself as "Calvin of the Trillin" (Mark Twain claimed to have served in the Confederate army with a man who spelled his name d'un'Lap). The selection by Mr. Keillor ("Shy Rights: Why Not Pretty Soon?") is less rich than such spookily moving pieces of his as "Drowning 1954" and "After a Fall," but shyness has a deep significance in the tradition of Benchley, Thurber, and White; and Keillor, in all due modesty, has faced shyness down.

Whether feverish or laid-back, Humor springs from a

certain desperation, which uses jujitsu on looming fear and shame, flirts almost pruriently yet coolly with madness and sentimentality, and fuses horse sense with dream logic. Asked about what it takes to write jokes, Woody Allen once replied, "That leap. I'm scared of dead patches."

Richler is a venturesome anthologist, and it is interesting that he found Humor in Naipaul, Saul Bellow, and Truman Capote. But how come Max Beerbohm isn't in this book? It is easy to carp about omissions from any anthology, and laughter is a personal matter. But Beerbohm knew laughter inside out. In an essay called "Laughter," Beerbohm recalled, from Boswell, the time that Dr. Johnson broke up over a will written by a Mr. Chambers:

"Certainly there is nothing ridiculous in the fact of a man making a will. But this is the measure of Johnson's achievement. He had created gloriously much out of nothing at all. There he sat, old and ailing and unencouraged by the company, but soaring higher and higher in absurdity, more and more rejoicing, and still soaring and rejoicing after he had gone out into the night."